The
MISSION MYTH

The
MISSION MYTH

BUILDING NONPROFIT
MOMENTUM
THROUGH BETTER
BUSINESS

DEIRDRE MALONEY

Business
Solutions
Press

San Diego, California

The Mission Myth: Building Nonprofit Momentum through Better Business

ISBN: 978-0-9840273-0-9 paperback
         978-09840273-1-6 ebook

Publishing consulting, project management and editing
by Karla Olson, BookStudio, www.bookstudiobooks.com

Copyediting by Lisa Wolff
Indexing by Ken Della Penta
Cover and interior design by *the*BookDesigners, www.bookdesigners.com

Printed in the United States of America

Published by

Business
Solutions
Press▬

113 West G Street, #647
San Diego, CA 92101
(619) 209-7749
www.makemomentum.com

Publisher's Cataloging in Publication Data

Maloney, Deirdre.

    The mission myth : building nonprofit momentum through better
    business / Deirdre Maloney. -- San Diego, CA : Business Solutions

    Press, c2012.

    p. ; cm.

    ISBN: 978-0-9840273-0-9 (pbk.) ; 978-0-9840273-1-6 (ebk)
    Includes index.

    1. Nonprofit organizations--Management. 2. Mission statements.
    3. Business planning. 4. Strategic planning. I. Title.

HD62.6 .M35 2012   2011938824
658.048--dc23   1202

DEDICATION

To the clients, staff and board members of Colorado AIDS Project,

who shared in seven years of lessons learned...

And to my husband and all-around favorite person, Jason,

who never let me whine too much as I learned them.

TABLE OF CONTENTS

PART THREE: Money

PART FOUR: Marketing

PART FIVE: Measurement

PART SIX: Wrapping It Up

INTRODUCTION

Welcome.

Chances are you've cracked open this book because you care about your nonprofit and you want to figure out how to run it better. Or maybe you're not yet running a nonprofit, but you want to know how to do so effectively. Or maybe you're at the end of your rope and you need a lifeline.

If you do currently run a nonprofit, I have a special message for you right now, first thing:

This job is hard. I mean really hard. I mean the tearing-up-your-stomach, clenching-your-throat, sleepless-nights kind of hard. And nobody but those who do it truly understands why.

I do. And so I'm here to help by first telling you that no matter how it feels sometimes, you are not alone. You are not crazy.

I'm also here to tell you that you're doing something great, but there are ways to do it better.

Thank you for taking the time to learn a few of the ways how.

Why I Can Talk about This

I got my first—and only—executive director job when I was fairly young.

Somehow, at 28 years old, I found myself running Colorado AIDS Project in Denver, the largest community-based HIV/AIDS provider in the state. At the time that I took on the position we had a budget of about $3.5 million, a staff of 40, and a long history of serving people living with this terrible disease while also working to prevent the spread of the infection to others.

Because I am both painfully realistic and a big believer in humility, I admit right up front that, although I did do a few things right to get that job, I actually got it for a whole lot of reasons that had nothing to do with me.

I was working as the marketing director at the organization when the position opened up. I'd been there about a year and a half, and during that time I had gotten to know the nonprofit well. During that time we'd gone through a number of changes—including a biggie. Our wonderful executive director of 18 years stepped down, and the board of directors launched a national search to replace him. We all held our breath, fingers crossed, in the hopes that our next leader would be the perfect person to take us to the next phase in our evolution.

The perfect leader lasted for five months. And when the board decided he wasn't the right fit for us, the organization went further astray. Though the board's decision to let him go was the right one, it was not easy to find ourselves without a leader—again, and so soon.

To make matters worse, at the time, the organization itself was suffering from some pretty common and dangerous challenges—the kind that most, if not all, nonprofits face at one time or another. The kind that we think nobody but other nonprofits could ever understand or endure.

We had just completed a rough fiscal year and, with no ED (from here on in my word for executive director, CEO, leader, what have you) in place, it was the board who took on the tough duty of cutting personnel to balance our new budget. The morale of those who remained was pretty low, as was their trust and opinion of the organization. The public's opinion of the organization? Not much better. We were struggling. We needed a leader.

Throughout the next several years I often wondered just what possessed me to throw my proverbial hat in the ring when the position opened up again. Since I was working at the organization at the time, I didn't have the excuse to say I didn't know what the challenges would be. I knew full well what lay ahead.

I like to think it was my deep desire to help the organization that led me to apply for the job—and for the most part it was. I truly did want to *do good* for a cause I cared about. And I truly believed I could do a good job. I'd be lying, though, if I said a bit of hubris didn't play into the decision as well. After all, I was vying to be the leader. And leaders have a lot of power.

And so I submitted my résumé. I told myself and anyone who asked that if I got the job it would be great. And if I didn't get the job it would be fine. And I believed this. The organization was in rough shape, and even from my inexperienced scope, it was clear that this job would not be easy.

And then...I got it.

I got the job because the board was scared. They had just hired an unknown, and it had backfired. I got the job because I was a known entity. They knew my strengths, they knew my weaknesses. They hoped there would be no more surprises. I got the job because there weren't a whole lot of other, great options. I got the job because I'm a marketer, and I gave a great presentation.

I ran the organization for seven years. I ran it through 72 board meetings and 150 executive staff meetings. I helped create seven budgets and assisted with seven audits. I appealed to each funder seven times. I oversaw seven AIDS Walks and seven galas. I coordinated the creation of two strategic plans, and seven years of their implementation. I worked with four board chairs, welcomed in dozens of new board members, and said good-bye to dozens more. I headed up a move to a new location and took on a strategic restructuring. I hired several staff members and let many others go. I made controversial decisions, learned from many, many mistakes, and celebrated enough wins along the way to keep me going.

I ate, slept, celebrated, and cried my way through seven years as an executive director. And I am confident that at the end of this lifetime, this particular job for this particular organization will go down as the most fulfilling, most exhilarating, most challenging, and most stressful time of my life.

Would I change any of it? Most often I say no. But it's easy to say that now that I'm on the other side. I learned a lot. And it got me exactly to where I am today, which is owning a company, speaking to audiences and writing books about how to run a nonprofit effectively while still getting a good night's sleep. Most of the time.

At the same time, my memory hasn't completely faded. That job was tough. Tougher than anything I'd ever endured…or have since.

And it began right from the start.

PART ONE

The
MISSION MYTH

Chapter 1

NONPROFIT? BUSINESS? BOTH?

When I first took over at Colorado AIDS Project, or CAP as I'll call it from here on in, it was a fun place to work. We had lots of passion and we worked each day for those who needed us. We did our best.

But…

We were also a multimillion-dollar nonprofit organization, and, like many nonprofits our size, hadn't strategically evolved, functioning as though we were still working out of the basement of a church.

There is a time and place for what I call "the clubhouse effect"— when everyone has a "pitch-in" attitude, gathering together for fundraising events or to stock the food bank or to write a grant. This time and place is when the organization is young and filled with volunteers. Once you get some money in the bank, some funding in the door, and some commitment to and from the community, the clubhouse effect simply does not work anymore.

We were lucky at CAP in the sense that our longtime executive director had kept our programs solid throughout his tenure. He saw the organization right from the beginning of the AIDS crisis, when CAP's role was to help people die with dignity, through the politically correct phase, when the money—and new levels of accountability—began to roll in. He also saw us through the late 1990s, when AIDS was faded from the spotlight and was replaced by other causes, and the organization found itself serving mostly the poor, homeless, and hungry who also happened to be living with HIV.

Three different organizations, three different sets of challenges and opportunities. This long-term ED navigated the organization through it all.

The problem was that although the programs were solid, there was still this sense that we were a grass-roots organization. But that was no longer the case. We'd taken on government funding by the millions, and expanded services to meet the emerging needs of our clients. We needed systems. We needed strong policies for our staff, a good Internet server, and a kitchen where we knew the microwave wasn't going to explode.

We weren't running like a business. And yet it couldn't be denied that, at our size and our scope, that's exactly what we had become, like it or not.

Crossing the For-Profit/Nonprofit Divide

Running a nonprofit like a business is not necessarily a popular approach.

I've seen it over and over again: Those who work in the non-profit sector look pretty negatively on their for-profit counterpart. They leave corporate America because they don't want to focus on chasing that proverbial dollar. They want to do something that "makes a difference." They see everything corporate as greedy and overly competitive, instead of giving and caring, like nonprofits.

To be sure, for some companies this is all true. But there's also another truth that some in the nonprofit sector don't see—and per-haps don't *want* to see.

Sometimes, for-profit businesses get things *right*.

Having goals to strive for, systems to get you there, policies that set parameters, and an understanding that politics always play a role -- each of these is not only positive, but critical for any orga-nization—for-profit or nonprofit—that wants to conduct business effectively. Just because the nonprofit "business" is focused on a purpose doesn't mean it can't—and shouldn't—ensure it runs with maximum impact. Maximum efficiency.

In fact, I'd argue that because nonprofits work toward a higher purpose, it is even more important that they do so.

When I began my journey as an ED, I somehow knew that my role at CAP would be to help the organization realize its business side. I knew that if we had clearly defined strategic goals, if we had the right people in the right seats, if we had the technical ability to capture information and report it, then our good nonprofit could become even better.

It didn't take me seven years to get there, but it took a while. It was hard work, and not nearly as fun as that clubhouse mentality had been. But in the end I can say definitively that the organization was better for it. And so were our clients.

How did I do it?

Read on.

Chapter 2

THE REAL, HARD TRUTH ABOUT MY ED JOURNEY

It's truth time.

The lessons you'll read throughout this book, the opinions I've gathered during my time in the nonprofit sector, the realities of leadership I've learned along the way—they almost all have one thing in common.

I learned them because I did them wrong the first time.

I like to consider myself a somewhat learned individual, which means I also like to think that I make each mistake only once. In some cases this was true about my time at CAP, but truth be told there were plenty of other instances when I had to go through the pain more than once before I figured out exactly why things weren't working out.

And I do mean pain.

Remember, I went through the budgeting process for my nonprofit seven times. I don't want to tally up how many of those budgets went awry before I finally figured out how to do it well.

I sat through dozens—no, hundreds—of board meetings. Same thing.

I oversaw a few strategic plans and joined many, many committees. Ditto.

I tried to organize my tasks, and I tried to communicate effectively. I had a lot to learn, and I did a lot of it on the fly. And in a lot of cases I did it wrong the first time.

What made the difference was that I was always aware of it. I knew I had to be humble, that I needed to recognize my mistakes. And so I swallowed hard and faced them head on. And it stung.

But here's another truth, and it might bring you some relief: None of my mistakes caused us to shut down. Even when I made them more than once, even when my mistakes seemed unfixable and it seemed as though I'd doomed our organization, they weren't and I hadn't. And after I fixed them, my organization was always stronger for it.

What I can also say is that it wasn't just my organization that was stronger as a result of the process. So was I.

I also spent those seven years morphing into a completely different kind of leader. I began as an analytical leader—carefully weighing the costs and benefits every time, checking with my topic experts every time, giving myself as much of a guarantee as I could that I was making the right decision. Every time.

In the end, I emerged with a whole different level of confidence. I didn't need to ask as many questions, and I didn't second-guess myself nearly as much. I still wanted to make the right decisions; I just didn't have to go through as much process to do so.

How Did I Get There?

It took some time, but I got better at the job. I got better at hiring staff and I got better at firing staff. I learned how to budget and to monitor financials. I learned why our marketing wasn't working and I realized how to make it more effective. I learned first what not to do with my board, and then what to do with it. I learned to be reasonable in my goal setting and effective in my execution. I learned how to communicate clearly—with everyone.

Perhaps most important, I took each lesson learned—painful and humbling as it was—and forced myself to grow. It meant swallowing a whole lot of pride. It meant many moments when I wondered just what the heck I was doing in this kind of position. It made me wonder if I was doing more harm than good.

But here's the good news.

I was in the position because, inherently, I *was* a good leader. I possessed raw leadership skills, I had a commitment to my organization, and I learned every day how to make things better.

So do you. And so I make you this promise.

Over time, if you keep making yourself better each and every day, you can't help but grow—exponentially. And your organization will be better for it.

One way to learn? Read this book and learn from me.

This book is filled with nuggets learned, not from a textbook or a conference on nonprofit management, but from facing real situations, dealing with them, and learning how I could have handled them better. These nuggets came from making mistakes. I now use them to help nonprofits, big and small, make fewer of them. My hope is that you'll make fewer of them, too.

Chapter 3

THE MISSION MYTH

And so we've arrived at my biggest lesson of all: the Mission Myth.

I begin with the common story, the one told by so many of us who began our careers in the for-profit world.

I was working for a for-profit company and I was disheartened by the constant focus on the bottom line. I decided to leave the corporate world behind so I could, to put it simply, do good.

We join nonprofits because of the mission, and we should. We love them for the same reason, and we should.

We immerse ourselves in them, pour our time, effort, and tears into them, all because of the mission—because we care about the good the organization does each and every day.

But here's the truth.

The mission may drive you. It may be the reason your organization exists, the reason people join it, staff it, volunteer for it, and give to it. It may be the thing that gets you up in the morning.

But...

It is *not* the reason an organization succeeds. In fact, in some nonprofits the mission is such a central, sole focus that it can drive the organization's focus *away* from results, *away* from success. Our relentless ambition to do more and more *good*, however we need to and at whatever cost, actually causes the organization to falter and, in some cases, fail.

We are doing good, but we are not doing good *well*.

And that's when we learn the truth: that the things that cause a nonprofit organization's success are often the very same things we couldn't stand about the for-profit world when we worked there.

I call them The Four Ms: Management, Money, Marketing, and Measurement.

These are not sexy principles. They are about running a business, and in the end they are just as important—and some cases *more* important—in determining whether or not a nonprofit organization is successful.

It may be the mission that drives you. But it's the business that drives you to success.

It's a hard fact for many in the nonprofit sector to swallow. Caring, passionate individuals don't become staff members at nonprofit organizations because they care about policies and procedures. They don't join boards because they care about governance.

In the beginning, when these individuals make the move to the nonprofit sector, puffing up their chests and knowing that their altruistic spirit is about to descend on an unsuspecting organization, they don't think about accounting. Or liability insurance. Or office space. These mundane details don't inspire passion.

As a result, it becomes all too tempting to disregard everything but the mission itself, to sacrifice capacity building or staff reviews or information technology in order to deliver another home-cooked meal, give another speech about environmental sustainability, or produce another theater show that will enhance the culture of the community.

When we succumb to these temptations we feel wonderful at first. Yet they must be resisted. Though they may seem like the exact things we should focus on, they in fact distract us from some of the most important elements of running an effective nonprofit.

To believe that mission alone will lead to success, to believe that the work must always be about your mission, to believe you must focus there and there alone, is a myth.

Focusing on your mission means you are doing good. It does not mean you are doing good *well*.

How to do good well? That's where The Four Ms come in.

Integrate them with your mission—make sure your nonprofit is running like a strong, solid business—and there's no telling what you can do, or where you might go next.

When we stand outside and view the nonprofit world, it's easy to idolize it—to think that because we are doing good work, the work itself is pristine and perfect.

But once we're in it we know it's not. It's messy and personal and wonderful and painful.

And, because we want to it to be successful, we also learn the truth: that a nonprofit is a business, and we must run it well.

I lived the Mission Myth. I took a job for the mission and dedicated my life to it. But in the end, it was my work with the four *M*s, my commitment to running it like a business and figuring out how to do so, that helped CAP do good *well*.

In the end, I realized that was my job.

Now, let's move on—to those Four Ms, and the lessons I learned about each one of them.

Remember, they came from pain. I urge you to read them, learn from me, use them, and save yourself a bit of heartache if you can.

HOW I LEARNED ABOUT THE MISSION MYTH

I came to the Mission Myth the way I came to many other lessons—the hard way.

I was working in the for-profit sector, and I had that pivotal moment, that change of heart that so many of us have right before we decide to make that altruistic sacrifice, to give our professional lives over to the nonprofit sector.

The truth is that my for-profit job—working as a local television news producer—was pretty cool, all things considered. That being said, it took just a few years for me to grow tired of, then frustrated about, the bureaucracy—the policies and the procedures, the office politics and the egos.

I told myself that the office life wasn't a good use of my time, that by focusing on silly issues like who would clean up the lunchroom and how to play nice with the intern meant we had all lost the meaning of what we were trying to do. I noticed a pattern. After all, this wasn't my first for-profit experience. I'd worked in retail and I'd scooped ice cream. I'd waited tables and sat at reception desks. Each job brought with it rules and regulations that seemed silly, bosses who didn't get me, and all kinds of tedious bureaucratic procedures.

Clearly the for-profit world wasn't for me.

And so one day I decided to give the nonprofit sector a shot. I knew that I would be more fulfilled if I was working toward a mission instead of a profit-driven goal, and I truly believed my worst day at a nonprofit would beat my best day at a for-profit for that reason alone.

That's when I began my search for my next thing, the thing that would fulfill my heart and use my talents for good.

It didn't take me long to find my first nonprofit landing pad, my first job in the sector. I dutifully accepted the position and took a pay cut, which only added to my rosy-cheeked vision of giving and sacrifice, and I showed up on my first day all puffed up, anticipating what it would be like to work in the nonprofit world and knowing, just knowing, this was where I belonged.

And in the end it was. But for very different reasons than I'd imagined. In the end I did get to do good, but not by serving food to the poor or housing the homeless. Instead, I did good through business relationships, political savvy, and following bureaucratic lessons—each of which I was able to do because I'd learned how from my work in the for-profit world.

Ironic, yes?

In the end, I did the most good for my nonprofit by being strategic and organized. By running the organization like a business, thinking about efficiencies and implementing those same policies and procedures I loathed in my previous for-profit jobs—the ones I soon learned actually made all the difference.

And here's the other thing I learned.

The office politics from my old gig? The constant managing of relationships and egos, the feelings of worthlessness, the personality conflicts? They were front and center in the nonprofit world, too.

PART TWO

MANAGEMENT

Chapter 4

WHAT MANAGEMENT REALLY IS

When we were kids and people asked us what we wanted to be when we grew up, we thought in terms of big, cool jobs—jobs we'd seen in the movies or on television, jobs like actor and doctor and astronaut.

Then, we get older. We begin to believe the best jobs are those with the most power, the most control. And so we want to become managers. We want to manage projects and people and organizations.

What Most People Think

In our minds, when we become effective managers, we will:
- have all of the say because we know best.
- be beloved by our staff because we know how to build a team.
- exceed all of our goals because we know how to focus and get stuff done.
- make lots of money—for ourselves and for our company.

The Truth

There's a reason you don't always like your boss, and it's not just because he or she has some flaws.

The truth is that when we become effective managers, we will:
- be disliked, and often hated, by many (and we should be).
- have to give up some power to get things done.
- make mistakes.
- lose sleep over money.

The Good News

It is possible to do management well.

Management of a nonprofit is absolutely critical to fulfilling its mission. When you do it right, you are achieving amazing things, getting results, making people's lives better.

And in the end, that's what it's all about.

Chapter 5

STRATEGY

Managing an organization well does not happen by chance. It takes drive and commitment to your organization, your staff, your board, and your programs.

Managing an organization well takes incredible organizational skill (see page 41), attention to detail, rigorous time management (see page 133), and the right kind of people skills (see page 165).

But the most important thing to know, the most important place to start, the most important thing you will need, is to focus on strategy.

Without strategy, your organization will simply not be as successful as it could be—for you, for your stakeholders, or for those you serve. Period.

For an organization to effectively meet its mission, it must first clearly define its goals. It must know what it is striving for. It must know that everything that occurs every day aims for something bigger. It must then lay out the objectives that will allow it to meet those goals.

When you're in the car and zooming toward a meeting, you take a specific road because you know exactly where you want to end up. You take it because you know it will get you there. You also know that sometimes there will be construction and detours, and sometimes you will run out of gas or need to course correct. But you are on a path to get to where you need to be. Which means you first figured out where you need to be.

There are those who believe that setting goals stifles creativity. That when you know exactly where you're going, you'll never wind up on those cool back roads, the ones that lead to all kinds of happy accidents, new restaurants, fun people.

And that's true. But you are not taking a trip to the back country; you are running a nonprofit. You must intentionally choose what you want to achieve and pinpoint the ways you expect to get there. You do not have the time or the money to wander around looking for happy accidents. That's not how businesses succeed.

And it doesn't stop there. Once you've set your goals for the year—or three years, or five—you then need to go deeper. You must create a work plan to achieve every objective, a timeline to guide you to the objectives efficiently, the measures that will inform you if you've met them, the communication strategy to keep everyone informed of the progress, and a schedule to revisit the whole thing regularly.

The plan must live and breathe. We all know that cliché—now just so *tired*—about the plan that collects dust on the shelf. This is not okay. Not on your watch. The plan must be monitored and reviewed regularly. It must be built strategically into ongoing meeting schedules. It must be talked about daily.

And here's the other thing many miss: the leaders of the organization need to be excited about it. They must:

- Refer back to the goals as new ideas and strategies arise, always looking to see how new brainstorms fit into the strategy.
- Communicate their excitement to everyone else.
- Create an environment where everyone looks ahead to a future of new achievements and can't wait to get there.
- And when they get there, they need to figure out where else they will go.

The mission itself is not enough. This is about remembering not just what you're working *for*, which is the mission, but also what you're working *toward*, which is what you will do *within* that mission to truly impact those you serve.

The Ampersand Mission

A warning about your mission: When I first took over as executive director at CAP and for most of the time that I was there, we had what I call an ampersand mission: to improve the lives of those living with HIV/AIDS and to prevent the spread of HIV.

We all believed it was a solid mission. It was a critical mission. And that was true.

Except that part about it being *a* mission. It was actually two missions.

When the organization was formed, there were virtually no HIV services in Denver. Everyone was still scrambling about, trying to figure this disease out. There was fear and panic and grief and loss. And so the organization took it all on—helping those living with AIDS, and providing information about the disease and how to prevent it.

By the time I took over in 2001, we were serving more than 1,500 people. And at the same time we were reaching out to different communities, all with targeted messages, trying to get them to understand AIDS and keep from getting it.

Both sides of the mission remained important. Both sides got bigger. And both sides had their own set of goals, challenges, funding, and staff.

Our AIDS programming was now two very different sets of programs, and as needs changed and budgeting issues cropped up, we found ourselves having to make all kinds of choices between them.

I don't believe we did anything wrong. We had the capacity to implement both missions in a way other organizations couldn't. Yet at the same time we were one agency running two missions, and there were times we had to choose between which one could grow, which one would need to be cut, and which one would get our greatest focus.

These weren't easy conversations, and I remember spending sleepless hours worrying that we would have to cut one at some point.

Why the sleepless nights? Because I was the leader, and I was invested in both missions. But leaders need to make hard choices.

I've seen the ampersand mission everywhere.

- I've seen environmental organizations work toward a better quality of life through everything from recycling programs to antipollution campaigns to advocacy regarding climate change.
- I've seen organizations focus on providing support to domestic violence victims while also sheltering those in poverty.
- I've seen organizations that produce expensive and beautiful orchestra shows also try to increase access to the arts for those who are less fortunate.

These organizations are not wrong. They are certainly not bad.

But the truth is that when you ampersand your mission—or even when it's not part of your mission but part of who you are—you dilute your focus. You dilute your message, and perhaps even confuse your stakeholders. You are doing good things, but you put at risk your ability to do them well.

In my work with nonprofits, especially those in their early stages, I see how often they struggle to make tough choices. They are so excited about their cause and all they can achieve. Yet it is critical that they be realistic about what they can *actually* achieve, and the dollars they have to achieve it. This means creating short-term goals that are reasonable for the resources they have, and looking to a future where they might expand to meet related needs—when they're ready. But for now, it means being focused and realistic, and communicating it all with great care.

It is not a bad thing to have a mission with an ampersand. Just know it when you do, and figure out how to prioritize when needed. Think about your true niche—the things you do better than anybody else. Think about the greatest needs. Be honest with yourself and own it. Make sure you can carry out both missions well. If you can't, you might need to choose one.

After all, no matter how hard we try, we can't be all things to all people.

Mission Creep

And another word of mission warning…

Even if we've got one solid, focused mission, there's another way almost all of us dilute our efforts. It's called mission creep.

I turn again to CAP, where we not only helped those living with HIV/AIDS and tried to stem the tide of HIV infection, but found ourselves tiptoeing into other arenas.

We toyed with the idea of taking on a hepatitis prevention program because many people living with HIV also live with that disease. We were approached about taking on an antismoking initiative because those living with HIV tend to smoke. We considered the idea of getting into the pregnancy prevention arena because many of the messages were similar to those for HIV prevention.

Why? Because we wanted to help, of course.

And—and let's be real here—because there was potential funding involved. Funding that would not only help support these new programs, but some of our existing staff and infrastructure as well. It was very tempting.

It will happen to you. You will lick your lips at potential funding that can come in the door to create a new program—one that isn't necessarily your mission, but one you can easily justify.

When this happens, at a minimum, acknowledge it. Own it. Have a discussion that honors the fact that your mission is creeping out, like a puddle on the sidewalk filled with rain. Remember those goals you set? (See page 35.) Bring them into the conversation.

Think about your messaging, and your constituents, if you expand outside. How will they feel? What will it mean to your brand? Then make an intentional decision.

There are also plenty of times when your decisions can still justifiably be part of your mission, but they're not part of your strategic goals.

I worked with one organization that followed this course of action regularly. Needing to bring in money, they responded to a call for funding to support a program that easily fit into their mission. Their mission was broad. Most missions are.

The problem? They weren't running that kind of program.

So what did they do? They *created* one because the funding was there.

It happens every day:

- An organization that helps nonprofits by providing quality accounting services begins to offer high-level office suites because a funder thought it would be a great idea.
- An organization focused on recycling creates a digital mapping program to pinpoint the region's pollution problems because a funder is hot on the topic at the moment.
- A nonprofit focused on early childhood development takes on job-training services for adults living with developmental disabilities.

Decisions to take on funding to create a new program should be made only after true, often hard discussion, after first reviewing the goals and being clear that the decision is the right one for the organization. Yet oftentimes this isn't what happens. Instead the decision is made without a whole lot of thought, and for one reason only—because there's money attached to it.

So be honest. Avoid new programs that don't fit your goals, even if your mission and your funder would both allow it. Stick to what you do well, what your organization is trying to achieve.

In the end, if you decide the new program is so important that you would do it even if there wasn't money attached, then change your goals and let everybody know that's why you're doing it. And then consider what area might lose some focus as a result.

It bears repeating: We can't be everything to everybody. We need to pick what we will focus on and do it well.

Chapter 6

THE IMPORTANCE OF SYSTEMS

My first day at CAP, a year and a half before I would move up and take on the ED role, was an exciting one. Actually, as I walked in the lobby that first morning I felt downright liberated. Like so many others, I had been working for a for-profit company and joined a nonprofit because I wanted to do something I could feel good about.

Fast-forward nine hours, when I came home from that first day and reported to hubby that I was now working at the professional equivalent of a dormitory. The building was falling apart. There was a lot of chitchat. Program supplies lined the hallways.

I admit, I found this environment somewhat refreshing after my time spent in corporate America. It was exactly what I'd expected, exactly what I'd always thought it would be, and exactly how many nonprofits (and many for-profits, for that matter) function.

Yet a part of me knew, even then, that something was missing. We didn't talk about our goals. We didn't follow policies and procedures. We spent our time wandering from task to task, meeting to meeting. We worked organically, without much structure.

None of this was necessarily bad. It didn't mean we weren't doing good work. It did, however, mean we weren't doing our *best* work.

And so, an exhilarating, challenging, somewhat tumultuous 18 months later, when I accepted the role of executive director, I decided to build on what we had—on our passion and our people and our mission—and make things even better.

It was not enough to do good. We needed to ensure our excellence.

Now I just needed to figure out how. Which I did, over many years, and after many mistakes.

What does achieving excellence *really* entail? Running an organization the way you would run a business.

For starters, the organization cannot run its day-to-day operations based on the people in the seats at the time, no matter how wonderful and committed they are. There must be systems in place so that no matter what happens, no matter who is there and who isn't, the organization achieves its goals efficiently and effectively. Systems set up the expectations, parameters, goals, and measurements for your organization. They create a mechanism for sustainability. They are your insurance policy.

Systems are how everyone functions in your nonprofit machine. They include well-thought-out policies and procedures for everything from human resources to volunteer recruitment, from ethics to who shuts off the lights at the end of the night.

Simply put, things need to work—work right, work efficiently, work *well*. Computers can't crash and sinks can't leak. Everything that gets done in your organization needs to be spelled out—briefly—with individuals designated for each task.

You might get pushback on this. I have. Many have. I've literally heard the words, *"Well, that's just not us. We don't have a policy for everything and we get our work done."*

Getting the work done is not enough. Nonprofits are obligated to get the work done well, to get it done right, to provide the best possible value to their stakeholders and to constantly improve themselves. If you don't have goals and objectives you're working toward, if you don't have policies and procedures in place to function each day, I guarantee you are not working as well you could—as you need to be.

Here's the other thing to know about systems, one of their most important benefits:

They make things less personal.

- When you have a system in place that says it's up to your supervisors to check the staff's timesheets and question comp time, then those supervisors are simply following required policy. It becomes less about Charlene questioning Steve about his timesheet, and more about what the supervisor is expected to do.
- When you have a policy that states that it's up to the volunteer coordinator to pick up the mail at the post office each day because you have limited resources, then you're not asking Daniel to do you a favor every day.
- When you have a board policy that says a member must give or get a certain amount of money every year, then following up with Amy on her donation is about the policy, not about calling her out for her lack of a monetary contribution.

This is especially important in the nonprofit sector, which can get pretty personal. It is filled with emotion and passion, which can then ooze out onto issues that aren't mission-related at all.

Systems create expectations, require consistency for an effective experience for all involved, sustain your organization, and make things less personal.

Systems emphasize that your organization must run well, and they clearly state how to get it to do that.

Now, here's the truth on systems.

Some people dislike them. And some people hate them. And some people loathe them.

- Some people feel systems suck the passion and the fun out of a nonprofit. Your answer? Systems will ensure your organization takes that passion and uses it for maximum good, every day.
- Some people feel you are reflecting the for-profit sector, an unfeeling, hard-nosed arena that doesn't care about people. Your answer? There are some things about the for-profit sector that are worth stealing.

- Some people know that systems actually make them a little less valuable. If all of a sudden you have a system in place that allows you to strategically delegate tasks, then those who get some value from stepping up and taking them all on will not be able to do so. If you have systems that preserve your history and clearly state how things need to be done, then your long-timers, with all of their institutional knowledge, won't be indispensible. Your answer? Systems will guarantee the organization survives after all of us move on. Isn't that what we all want for the organization?

None of these people are bad. They are great. They are passionate. They are emotional.

And that's why it's up to you as a leader to explain to them why systems are important, and why, no matter what, those systems are here to stay.

Chapter 7

THE FOUNDER

I'm about to step into some sticky territory—and it's all about the organization's founder.

It cannot be denied that founders are amazing people. They are incredibly committed. They are in love with the cause. They care so deeply about it, in fact, that they put a significant amount of time, energy, and sweat into forming the nonprofit and getting it moving forward. Back before the organization was even formed, chances are they spent extensive amounts of time thinking about it, crafting the mission, getting the legal forms together, and advocating to friends, family members, and anybody who would listen as to why they should get involved. Founders are absolutely, passionately in love with their organizations.

Wow! That kind of commitment is inspiring, unmatched by pretty much everybody else. And chances are it led to all kinds of successes for the organization—especially in those early years.

But...

That same passion, that same commitment, has a downside.

- Founders can feel so passionate about the organization they've created, so connected to the mission they've painstakingly crafted, so in love with the strategies they've set up, that veering from any of these in any way is just not an option. Ever.
- Founders often feel they know the organization better than anybody, that they alone truly *get* its work and its purpose—which means others who try to get in the way simply *don't* get it.

- The founder's identity is often intertwined with the organization itself, so that any changes to it, any insinuation that things aren't working well, any ideas of how to do things better, means the *founder* isn't working well, and could be performing better.

Working in a nonprofit, for a mission you love, is personal enough. Founding one is as personal as it gets.

The funny thing is that founders often understand founders' syndrome as a concept. In fact, I've gotten to know founders who talk about this phenomenon at other organizations and sadly shake their heads, wishing the leaders would just take a step back and realize how they're holding their nonprofits back. But when the topic turns to their own organizations, the ones experiencing the very same things? These same people deny anything is wrong.

It's a tricky dynamic for staff members, board members, and others who get involved and get in the way of the founder.

Often, change is necessary to move the organization to the next level, to make it more effective, to fix what's not going well. But the founder resists, gets defensive.

What happens next? Nothing.

Because this is personal. Because the nonprofit sector is filled with nice, great people who don't want to hurt feelings, who feel terrible devaluing a founder and the work he or she has put into the organization.

So what can organizations in this position do?

If you're a founder:

- First, know the truth. You've done something amazing.
- Second, acknowledge that this *something amazing* is not a part of you, and it will need to grow, to assume its own identity, to change.
- Third, take care to examine the role you've played in the organization's success.

- Next, examine whether you might be hindering its forward momentum by resisting change or shutting down when others make suggestions.
- Then, swallow hard, lower your defenses, and examine it again.

If you need to address this issue with a founder:

- First, know the truth. The founder has done something amazing.
- Second, know that you have, too. You've committed your time and energy to a nonprofit and to helping achieve its mission.
- Third, know that the founder issue is a messy one that needs to be addressed—addressed with care, yes, but addressed nonetheless.
- Next, find the person the founder trusts most and have this person help craft the message that things need to move forward. That things need to change. That you need to build on the foundation the founder put so much time and energy toward building. Have that person help deliver it.
- Then, stay strong. Your message might not be received well, but the fact is this is no one person's organization. Engage others to repeat the message and hold all people—founder included—accountable to the strategies created for the organization. Bring in an outside facilitator if needed.
- Finally, be kind—to the founder and to yourself. Founders deserve to be acknowledged for their hard work. And so do you—for having a hard conversation and making sure the organization functions as effectively as possible.

Chapter 8

THE BOARD OF DIRECTORS

Now that we've begun tackling some tricky territory, let's jump in with both feet, shall we?

When I was getting ready to start my own company, I talked to hundreds of nonprofit leaders to learn about their greatest challenges. What kept them up at night? What was taking up space in their heads? What was their most difficult thing to manage?

What they were very comfortable saying out loud —first thing—was the topic of money. Makes sense.

But just as common was the second thing they listed. Only this one was always mentioned a bit under their collective breaths, as though they were telling some kind of big secret.

Their second greatest challenge was their boards.

And my response to them was always the same: That secret is out.

Having worked for a board and served on many of them, I can honestly say that board members and their relationships with staff are, by nature, almost always guaranteed to land you smack dab in the midst of conflict and tension. And, really, it's not the board's fault.

Board issues are everywhere. *Everywhere.* Who is in charge of what in an organization? What, exactly, is a board member's job? Aren't board members supposed to raise money and be the good guys? (We go deep into this in the money section. See page 193.) Why don't they seem to know that? But aren't they also supposed to hold everybody accountable and be the bad guys? Why don't they seem to know that either?

I've done a lot of work in this arena, and have come to one true reality.

The problem begins with this nonprofit sector of ours. It sets up the board—and often the staff—from the very start.

Think about it.

You take a group of well-intended volunteers, who, remember, join an organization because they have a passion for the *mission*, not board governance.

You then bring them together at regular intervals to figure out how to govern an organization, when it's the staff who are there every single day and know the ins and outs of the organization.

Then you give these volunteers ultimate fiduciary responsibility, a term that is often not even defined for them when they take on this critical role.

I pause here to define it.

A fiduciary agent is a person or group of people to whom property or power is legally entrusted for the benefit of another.

It's pretty heavy stuff—heavy stuff that most board members don't even think about when they join. Instead, they join because they care about the mission. Or because someone they care about asks them to do so.

Why would they know about fiduciary responsibility? Why would they know that it's actually their mortgages on the line should the organization go awry? (The very reason board members must always ensure the organization has sufficient insurance before agreeing to join.)

Boards are required. Fiduciary agents are required.

But—and here's the big problem—establishing the system, how the board members will work with the staff and each other, is not.

It's a recipe for major problems—for organizational chaos and resentment on both sides. For the board, it often leads to issues like groupthink, conflict avoidance, lack of focus, strife with their executive director, and tedious meeting agendas. No wonder far too many boards look around the room at the start of their regularly scheduled board meeting and wonder if they'll make quorum. And then don't.

What's in it for them if they attend? Scouring over financials they don't understand? Tiptoeing around the give-or-get issue? Trying to get their personal agendas met while not stepping on the executive director's toes?

The thing to know is that, by its very nature, board governance comes with tension:

- Tension between caring about the mission and governing it correctly.
- Tension between not wanting to talk about numbers, yet having those pesky financials attached to every board packet.
- Tension between the executive director hired by the board to run the organization and the board members themselves, who believe there might be a better way to do things. Who—let's be real—sometimes join because they truly believe they know better.

How do you work through the many tensions organically created by the simple and required creation of a board? How do you make a board experience a functional, pleasant one for members as well as staff?

There are two pieces to this seemingly impossible puzzle: systems and selection.

Systems

Let's start with systems.

We've talked about this when it comes to managing the organization. (See page 41.) As with everything else, you need to design a machine within which you can function. Once you know your system and have determined your parameters, you then have the ability to be creative, adapt to new challenges, think bigger. But if you don't have that system in place first, you are flying blind and you won't be as successful.

What does building your board machine entail?

- Know everybody's role, board and ED included. Create a job description that clearly defines everyone's responsibilities and accountabilities.
- Get specific about the board's role in fundraising and its give-or-get expectations. (See page 193.)
- Clearly define the goals/strategies for the year, and how the board will monitor the organization over time.

Design policies and procedures that clearly outline everything from how the board will fulfill its fiduciary obligations to how it will work with the ED and how it will function itself as a body. These documents will set everything in motion and make everything less personal.

Make sure good bylaws are in place and updated to fit your organization. These are a big part of your board machine and will clearly lay out many of the policies already mentioned, such as attendance requirements, voting procedures, and annual meeting expectations.

A final word on the reason for systems—and it will sound familiar.

I have watched extremely successful for-profit executives enter the nonprofit board meeting context and lose every ounce of business-minded logic they had. Why? Because they joined for the *mission*, not because they were dying to be involved in messy business issues, and certainly not because they were jazzed to be fiduciary agents of an organization. Board members are passionate, emotional people too.

The harsh truth for many board members is that unless the nonprofit is small and the board considers itself a working board (not a governing board, which we are discussing now), it's *not* the board's job to run the mission.

But...

It's often what they want.

Remember the definition of a fiduciary agent? It means the board is actually working on behalf of the community to make sure everything works correctly, ethically, transparently, and toward the goals that they helped set. They must manage the organization's liability and ensure the organization's sustainability. They must know that people are being served as intended, that the money is being spent with integrity.

They do this by monitoring the systems.

A final note on setting up your board machine: Seriously consider an outside facilitator to help with this process. My organization used one to help us determine just what kind of nonprofit we wanted to be, then how to hold ourselves accountable to that vision through policies and procedures. Bringing in an expert from the beginning meant we had an objective facilitator who helped us stay on track, checked in on our work, and served as a guide when we got stuck. This expert was worth every penny and more.

Once you've done your homework, once you've clearly identified your board's role, determined which policies and procedures you need to include or update, taken a good look at your bylaws, and figured out how to make them relevant to your organization today, the work is not over. You must then function within your machine—and you must do it well, despite the many personalities, passions, and reasons for joining that come with each individual board member.

How do you get there? Get the right people. It's the second step in creating a functional, enjoyable board experience: selection.

Selection

You've gotten your systems in place—hurrah! No, really. Know that you're ahead of the pack and pat yourself on the back.

Now it's time to face the next critical step: getting the right people on your board, finding those crucial individuals who believe in your machine and who are invested in it enough to make sure it runs effectively within the parameters you've set.

This is a critically important step. Even if you've got the greatest board in the world right now working within the greatest system, it doesn't mean much if it falls apart next year when new people fill the seats. That's why board recruitment is another make-or-break moment for every ED, every board, and ultimately, every organization.

Here are some steps on how to do it:

Step 1: Develop a board job description.

Take this document seriously. Create it by thinking through what the board's role will be (governance) and what it will not be (event planning). Think through the time and money commitments you truly want and expect. Strategize what demographics and areas of expertise you want represented and create a board matrix to establish it. (There are templates available online.) Be thoughtful, clear, and honest about what you want your board to do—to *be*.

Step 2: Recruit accordingly.

Once you've figured all of this out, talk to prospects who fit the board you have designed. Do not bring on a board a member who wants to work at your food bank or who stands to have connections that will get your event catered at a lower price. And, as much as it might tempt you, don't bring on board members for the sole reason that they have money, friends with money, or both. (See page 198.)

Instead, recruit board members who understand your organization, and ideally who understand what fiduciary responsibility is in the first place. Practically speaking, recruit board members who can make your board meeting dates and times, and who understand up front your give-or-get policy. (This may sound obvious. Trust me, it isn't.)

Step 3: Make the vote an honor, not a given.

Board members should feel they have been accepted into something special when they make it onto your board. Don't make it a given that everyone who's up for the vote, or anyone who's interested, for that matter, gets on your board. (Don't do what I saw one organization do and vote on new board members while those candidates are sitting in the room. No lie. Take a wild guess as to how many people didn't get voted on.)

Be selective and think of what you need now and into the future. If you have board terms, know who is coming to the end of theirs and plan for their succession.

Do not tell people they should be on your board because it will be easy, or because it won't cost them a lot of time or money. That's not how you inspire. You inspire when you:

- Tell people about the great goals you are aiming toward in the coming years.
- Talk to them about the amazing work of the organization and the impact it has on people's lives.
- Tell them that they can be a part of it all by committing to this critical role.

They will follow your lead. Make it a joke and they will think of it as a joke. Make it an honor and they will feel honored.

It's up to you. But I ask you: Which is a more respectful way to treat your organization and those who are already committing themselves to it?

If you are begging people to join your board or allowing anyone with a pulse on it, you've got a big problem. Board recruitment is just as important as staff recruitment. It doesn't matter that board members are volunteers. What matters is that they play an incredibly important and challenging role, and they must illustrate their understanding of that role and their commitment to your organization before being permitted on the board. They need to understand this is a two-way street, and both sides need to feel comfortable that this is the right fit.

Pay attention to the questions potential board members ask and make sure they reflect an understanding of what you do. They should care enough about it to commit themselves to their roles, but also be willing to step back and let staff do their thing.

Know that sometimes a potential board member is simply not the right fit, and that is perfectly okay. As with staff recruitment, it is much better to figure out in the beginning that the fit isn't there and part ways graciously than to spend precious time and energy trying to work out an unworkable situation.

Step 4: Set them up for success.

Once you have the right people in the right seats, the job is not over. After they are voted in, offer them your hearty congratulations, then provide an orientation for them immediately.

Would you sit staff members in front of a computer on their first day and hope that they just figure things out? What kind of experience would that be? What kinds of outcomes would result? For everyone to be successful, new board members need to understand how the organization works, the part they play in it, how to read the organization's budget and financial statements, and the expectations around board meetings and the organization's events. They must get to know their executive director and understand that relationship. They must know that they will all be held consistently accountable to board expectations by the board chair.

Make sure you also provide ongoing training for the board—covering everything from their role as board governors to marketing, advocacy, public speaking, and fundraising. Bring in an expert to discuss the latest legislative issues impacting your cause or the nonprofit sector as a whole. Set your board members—and therefore your organization—up for success by arming them with the information they need to be effective.

A WORD TO THE ED ON SELECTION

When I first became an ED, I thought board recruitment was not an appropriate place for me to spend time. I also didn't happen to have a lot of extra time to spend, and so I let the nominating and executive committees handle this area.

It was one of my biggest mistakes.

I knew my organization extremely well, probably better than anyone else, because I was there in the trenches each and every day. Why in the world would I not extend this knowledge to help bring on appropriate board members? And why the heck did I think it okay to leave the selection of my more than a dozen bosses up to chance? And who on the board really had the time to make sure we were getting the right members on our board at the right time?

Seven years later, nobody got on our board—nobody even got to a meeting with our chair or nominating committee—without first meeting with me. The board understood that I knew the organization and could help define it to those who were interested in joining us. They also trusted me to be the first line of vetting so that they could focus on those who really were potential members.

I took this part of the job seriously. I didn't manipulate candidates or bring on only those who agreed with my points of view. I was able to articulate what a governing board truly was, how it meant that they wouldn't be involved in our day-to-day activities. I explained to them the system we'd set up, the way our board meetings worked, and the expectation that they would be our greatest ambassadors to the outside world. Those who made it to the next round were excited and hopeful that they would be accepted. And because I'd weeded out those who wouldn't have been the right fit, they often were. Another benefit? I was able to begin building my relationships with board members early.

It was not only beneficial for me to play this role, but a part of my *job*. If your board leaders don't agree with the role you should play in board recruitment, find others on your board who do and have them help bring about this understanding.

Trust me—it will make all the difference for you, your ability to do your job, and your organization's overall effectiveness.

Board Leadership

This next topic is one of *the* most important factors in board success: the people who lead it.

If board members need to be the right fit for your organization, if they must understand their role in board governance and fiduciary responsibility, then your board leader must excel at it.

Board chairs must understand that the organization needs to run with systems in place, must lead and inspire members to work within those systems, and must have the ability and the stomach to communicate directly when their fellow board members fall outside of appropriate parameters.

Conflict avoidance is as common on boards as it is for staff (and in life, no?). No matter. Just because people are volunteering to sit on a board does not mean they have free rein to do what they want, say what they want, have their own agenda, and run rogue. It is for the board chairs to run their boards and meetings with integrity, excellent communication, and an understanding of the critical role a board plays for an organization.

Board Succession

Two final words on the board, and they are just as crucial as the rest of them: succession planning.

As with the board in general, the greatest board leader in the world will do only so much good for an organization if the next person in line botches everything up.

In the same way the ED guides the organization's operations, the board chair determines whether or not the board—and in many ways, the organization—experiences wild success or terrible failure. The board needs to think ahead, starting when they recruit new members, as to who might play the critical roles of chair, vice chair, and treasurer. Succession of board leaders cannot be discussed for the first time during the month preceding (or the month of) the election. You should not have to beg someone to step into the role of chair. There should be no arm-twisting and no joking involved. The role of board chair should be taken seriously and intentionally. This person must be someone who has the vision to guide the organization, the ability to lead discussions among diverse members, the stomach to discuss uncomfortable issues, the humility to mitigate his or her own personal investment, and the knowledge that the role he or she plays—and the role of the board—is serious business. Yes, *business*.

DOES YOUR BOARD NEED SOME WORK?

Most do in some way.

If your board experience is not a functional, effective, enjoyable one, know that you're not alone. This problem is common.

At a minimum, a training on board governance is probably in order. You might also benefit from facilitated discussion to get at the root causes of why it's not functioning well and develop a plan to fix them.

If you are a board member and your board does not function well, if the experience is so frustrating that you are tempted to skip each and every meeting, it is your responsibility to talk to your board chair. If you are a board chair and you cannot lead your board with a focus on governance and policy, if you don't have it in you to hold your board to the highest of governance standards, consider resigning. This is too important.

Notice that I didn't say any of this was the executive director's role. I've seen EDs who were expected to manage their board issues, and it's an unfair, no-win situation every time.

Chapter 9

THE ED/BOARD RELATIONSHIP

I cannot think of any relationship more critical to the success or failure of an organization than that of the board chair and the executive director. If it's a true partnership, complete with clarified roles and responsibilities, mutual respect, and clearly defined parameters of communication and accountability, the organization can function well. If, however, one or more of the pitfalls I've seen over and over play into this relationship, the organization is in a precarious position. And this is common.

A healthy partnership requires a board chair who trusts that the executive is running the organization effectively and transparently. As for the executive director, he or she must feel supported, and be willing to provide information to the board chair without feeling defensive or threatened.

Board chairs and EDs don't need to be best friends. In fact, they don't even need to like each other all that much. What matters is that they respect and trust each other, that they understand and agree on their various roles, that they communicate well, and that they are willing to work together toward the goals of the organization. Ideally, neither has ego in the game, and both are acting for the good of the organization above all else. Also ideally, the board chair is an excellent and humble professional and the executive director is, too.

Step by Step to Synergy

Based on my experience, this is a tall order. So we might need to take this in baby steps. How do you get to a healthy and fruitful partnership between these two entities?

Step 1: Find the right board chair.
I've already said it: This position is make-or-break for an ED.

As the leader of the fiduciary agent of the organization, the person to whom the rest of the board will look for guidance, vision, and support, and the person who serves as a major accountability mechanism for the ED, a significant amount of responsibility rides on that person's proverbial shoulders.

Create a job description specific to this position, outlining the duties around the monitoring of board commitments, running of board meetings, upholding of bylaws, relationship to the ED, et cetera. Then find the right people to fill it.

Carefully thought-out succession planning and strategic thought must be done ahead of time to ensure the right person has the time, commitment, skills, and interest to play this critical role in an organization. And, as I've suggested, the board chair also needs a strong stomach, a good dose of humility, a lack of hidden agendas, and excellent communication skills.

I've said it before, but it bears repeating: *The board chair cannot be recruited in the minutes leading up to the meeting when the election takes place.*

Yet I've seen that happen over and over.

Don't do what so many others have done and make the big argument that taking on the role of board chair won't take *that much time.* The board chair needs to know the role, respect the ED, be willing to speak up with the group, and hold peers accountable. This leader needs to be immune to groupthink and be excellent at conflict resolution.

Step 2: Create the system.

The two most logical professionals in the world won't be able to function successfully if they don't know what they are supposed to be doing, so get the machine in place. (See page 50.)

A functional system makes that whole, potentially messy board/executive relationship more professional and less personal. It avoids unstated expectations, assumed intentions, and passive aggression. It's no longer about Dan as the chair and Sue as the executive and how they function together. It's simply about the chair and the executive.

Step 3: Drop the scapegoating.

It's a temptation that many can't resist. Something goes wrong, and you blame the other guy. I've seen executive directors blame their boards for staff reductions, budget cuts, and structural changes they had nothing to do with. I've seen them tell staff members that the board wouldn't allow raises or was forcing controversial personnel policies so that they wouldn't have to own the decision.

I've also seen board members blame the ED for problems within the organization, when ultimately, they themselves weren't paying enough attention. They can point to the staff all they want when the year ends in the red or when the organization loses funding or gets sued by a terminated employee. But they should know that they have played a big role in the problem, simply by not having the correct parameters, monitoring, and accountability mechanisms set up. And because they weren't paying enough attention or asking the right questions.

Blaming organizational problems on each other to the staff or to the external community, even when the fault clearly lies on one side, not only breaks trust between the two parties, but it reflects terribly on the organization. Why publicize organizational problems for everyone—clients and donors and volunteers—to see? To save face? Avoid a bruised ego? It's not worth it. Nobody likes it when bad things happen on their watch, but everyone asked for their role. This is the consequence to all that glory.

Step 4: Get along...but not too well.

Mutual respect and even admiration are critical to the board/ executive relationship, but don't let it go too far. Get along too well and know you'll create all kinds of rumors (perhaps true) about conflicts of interest and favoritism. Think it would be fun to go out for drinks with your board chair? Don't. You may say too much and regret it. Think you should treat your ED to dinner and a show, just the two of you? Don't. The last thing you want is for everyone else to think there is no accountability, that the new mission of the organization was designed over an intimate evening, or that a friendship has clouded the judgment of either of you about the reality of what's going on in the organization.

This can be a hard temptation to resist—especially because you have in common your passion for the mission. It's especially hard for the ED to avoid because there is so much to potentially gain from a close relationship with board members. Resist it anyway.

When board chairs and EDs function well together—without ego, with the best of intentions for the good of the organization, with open communication and a willingness to share the strengths and challenges; when they understand each other's roles and treat each other as the professionals they are, when they have no covered agenda and are appropriate in their relationship—the organization is well on its way to excellence.

A tall order? You bet. Impossible? Not at all. A work in progress? Almost always.

LEARN FROM ME: HOW I SCREWED UP MY RELATIONSHIP WITH MY BOARD, AND THEN GOT IT RIGHT

When I first took over at my organization, I was young, the board was fried, and all I wanted was for them to get out of my business so I could just set about fixing the organization. I had this kind of attitude for a few reasons.

Having terminated the executive director right before me, the board had gotten used to some fairly heavy involvement in our operations, which at the time was necessary. We had no captain on our proverbial ship and we were majorly adrift. Our financial picture was dim and we had to cut staff to stabilize. As an organization we could no longer deny that our machine was broken.

The second thing the board did was step into the operating side of the organization while recruiting a new ED, to the extent that the board chair stepped down from his role on the board temporarily to fill in as interim executive director.

By the time I took over, the staff had grown extremely anxious and so had I. We were admittedly and naively fearful that the board would never step out of their newly immersed role once they got a taste of the fabulous power. At the same time, I was faced with a board of 17 members, all of whom knew they were giving me a pretty big shot, all of whom considered themselves my mentors . . . all 17 of them.

So I came up with a brilliant solution. It not only showed the staff that I heard their concerns about board micromanagement, it also established me as the new boss and let the board know that I wasn't into too many directives.

I shut them out.

I gave them updates on a need-to-know basis, I controlled every message that landed in their in-boxes, and I went into board meetings on the defensive, ready to stand up for myself and my staff should they try to haggle their way into our business. Basically, I treated them like the enemy.

This not only was unfair and untrue, but it backfired. By holding the board members at arm's length, all I did was validate distanced behavior and limited involvement. I encouraged them to stand far aside, so much so that I left my organization without appropriate accountability and my staff with no support from this critical body of people. And as fried as they were when they first named me as ED, it only got worse. Since I didn't involve them enough, the board's level of engagement dipped even lower over the next several months. Board meetings were painfully tedious, as members began to forget what the organization was really all about. We wound up spending our meetings focusing on one of the least favorite topics of all, money—specifically the financials I hadn't yet fixed and the income I hadn't yet figured out how to get.

And I left myself hanging out there alone—supporting the staff, engaging the community, trying to make ends meet, firing people, hiring people, and wondering why I was feeling so completely isolated.

It was my fault, and it went on for two long years.

Even as we started moving forward as an organization and finding some success, the board was still behind. Their energy was low. They focused solely on financials and couldn't make quorum. Trust was low. Meetings were painful, tedious, condescending.

But this story has a happy ending. Things got better—slowly. By the time I left seven years later, I was working with board members who were truly engaged, who felt their time was being respected, who showed up for meetings and were excited to be a part of all that we were doing. We had mutual trust. We had committed people. We had systems. And as a result, our organization was able to achieve a whole new level of success.

I tell you EDs now: It's possible to have a great relationship with your board. And no matter what the board dysfunction—whether they are checked out or micromanaging or fighting or getting too close as a group—there are ways to fix it. I promise.

Here are some strategies you can start using now, based on my experience:

Strategy 1: Get to know them.

I did this by meeting with each board member separately. Even though there were a lot of them, and even though it took a lot of time, and even though I had to meet some out in the eastern part of the county and some at the crack of dawn for breakfast, I met with each and every one. It not only allowed me to build a relationship with all members by learning about them as people, but it also illustrated that I was more than the ED they saw in the board meeting—the one they perhaps saw as trying to take control, the one who didn't always engage them, the one who had to dance that political board dance so carefully that she couldn't go too deep during our discussions.

As we got to know each other better, as we began to build trust, they got more engaged in the organization. After all, I lived and breathed it. I truly loved being its advocate, and even though the board was already supposed to be there with me, I had made that nearly impossible. Over time, I could begin to call on the members individually for various needs, and to get feedback. And that's where Strategy 2 came in.

Strategy 2: Let them in. For real.

After several months of keeping the board members at arm's length—or farther—because I thought I needed them out of my business, and because I didn't want them hounding me while I figured out how to be the right kind of ED, I realized how much damage I had done. My efforts to keep them from micromanaging me had resulted in ambivalence. And so I made a conscious effort to bring them back, not only because I wanted them to support me and the organization but because it was the right thing to do.

You need a board that cares about the organization, members who can speak about it with others at a dinner party and are proud to do so. They are the fiduciary agents, the ultimate accountability mechanism, and they need to understand what that means, then honor it. To keep them at bay is to do a disservice to the organization and to them.

Admittedly, I also let them in because I began to have my own wins and establish myself in the community. I had built up some confidence and could more easily show them that I knew what I was talking about. I let them in because they had good, helpful things to contribute to the organization. I let them in because we began to establish trust. I let them in because—I had to admit it—I couldn't make it without them.

Letting them in meant I told them more about what was going on, including my mistakes and my challenges. I still brought plenty of solutions to each and every problem, but at least they knew the true picture of what we were facing as an organization.

Strategy 3: Fix your finances.

Our organizational picture was less than promising when I first took over. We were unstable—not just because we had a hard time getting the money in, but because we had an even harder time accounting for it when it got there.

I tried to hire great finance directors onto my team, but found I didn't even know the right skill set to recruit into the organization. And when they didn't last I was left with an ever-worsening financial situation, and no true sense of how to go about fixing it.

So I swallowed hard and I fixed it. I found the money and brought in two consultants to accurately reflect our financial information in our accounting software. It was expensive, but worth it. They not only clarified the previous year's books and prepared us for the upcoming audit, they also set up systems so that the next person in the position would be set up for success.

Despite these successes, I knew I needed to take one more step. In order to be truly confident in the process, I needed to get my own skill set in line. And so I decided to take the plunge: I went back to school to get my master's degree. I signed up for an Accounting for Nonprofit Managers class immediately, and I read the textbook cover to cover. I asked literally hundreds of questions in class, and I finally overcame the financial learning curve. Could I create a balance sheet? No. But could I read one, analyze one, and know what questions to ask so that I could then be prepared for the board discussion? You bet.

By working on this deficiency I was able to build trust with the board, who, much to their relief, didn't have to fixate on the financials so much anymore. I understood the financial statements, could explain them, and had solutions prepared for the lower-than-expected revenue and higher-than-expected expenses. Why? Because I knew what to look for. Because it was my job.

Strategy 4: Create a system.
As I mentioned earlier in this section, setting up the machine is absolutely key to board success. Ours took about a year to create, and we set about doing it diligently. We brought in an outside facilitator to help us determine the strategy for our systems, including the policies and procedures we'd need to create, the board/executive job responsibilities we needed to define, the bylaws we'd need to update, and the process we would go through to get it all done. We created a yearlong calendar to pinpoint which pieces we'd attack at each board meeting, and how we would use our annual retreat to comprehensively think through and track the organization's strategic plan.

One year later we had progressed exponentially—as a board/executive team and as an organization. We all knew what we were supposed to be doing, and we knew how we would be monitored throughout the year. As a team we knew we weren't leaving things to chance, and the board knew it was carrying out its fiduciary duties without having to fixate on the operational minutia. We had clearly established lines between governance and management, and we had great board meetings, thanks to an agenda template and board calendar that kept members engaged appropriately, and a set of guests that kept their energy and enthusiasm high.

Strategy 5: Get involved in board recruitment and succession planning.

I've said it before: If you are an ED, the worst thing you can do is leave new board members or board officers to chance.

After I learned this the hard way, by leaving to chance who my many bosses would be and—even worse—who my chair would be, I got smart. I began to assist our nominating committee, actively engaging in the dialogue of what skill sets and personality traits we were looking for, helping to identify potential members, and sitting in on recruitment meetings.

In the beginning I wasn't sure it was even my place to do so. But it was.

And so I took on a lot of recruiting work, using my various pieces of knowledge and also saving the board members a lot of time. They were still involved, of course, but so was I. And the board was glad to have me collaborate.

That's what happens when you build trust. That's what happens when you let board members in.

And with every new member, I kept an eye out for future chairs. And I started the dialogue early.

Chapter 10

SUPERVISING YOUR STAFF

So many of us, and I include myself in this, have always aspired to move up, up, up. We were taught growing up—through our families, through our schooling, through the media, or through a combination of all three—that a steady upward incline in a company means that we are successful. That we are honoring our skills. That we are *somebody*.

This upward movement means more money, more responsibility, and—let's face it—more power. And what is one way we are going to get more power?

We are going to supervise other people.

And we look ahead with gleeful anticipation! For many of us—especially those in the nonprofit sector—personnel management seems like such a wonderfully altruistic and mutually beneficial concept.

Through staff supervision, we will work with individuals who will surely be as committed to their work as we are to ours, who will think the same, talk the same, and hold the same values and priorities that we do. We will bestow on these staff members all of the wisdom and knowledge we've collected over the years, and they will be grateful for it, soak it up like a sponge, and perform even better as a result.

And then, after all of the enthusiastic daydreaming, we actually *become* supervisors. And it doesn't take long for us to realize what a fantasy each and every part of that whole idea really was.

While supervision can indeed be very fulfilling, it's also really, really tough—if it's being done right, that is.

Do it in the nonprofit sector and it only gets tougher.

Why?

Because of the Mission Myth.

Because people who join the nonprofit sector are in it for the mission. They are in it because they care, because they are passionate about the cause and the organization's role in it. Because they want to put their efforts, their daily lives, into *doing good*.

I pause here for a quick illustration.

When I first took over as ED, staff morale was...not so great. One of my strategies to address this was to bring in an outside facilitator to do some team-building.

He started by asking us to divide into three groups: head people, heart people, and gut people. We were told to think about where we first went when we digested something new, when we had to make a decision, when we interacted with people.

There were about 40 of us. As we divided up and looked around the room, here's how it shook out:

- 3 head people
- 3 gut people (including me)
- 34 heart people

And I don't think our organization was unique. In fact, I've worked in the nonprofit sector enough to know we weren't. It was pretty much spot-on.

And this is the beauty of the nonprofit sector. It's also the curse for nonprofit supervisors.

Make no mistake, nonprofits are filled with smart people. Their reasons for joining your organization are about putting those smarts into the organization, into the mission. Which also means that for them, this is more than a profession.

This is personal. And that means everything—every conversation, every change, every piece of feedback—has the potential to be personal as well.

Seemingly benign policies and procedures, cuts that need to be made to sustain the organization, honoring the needs of the funder in order to get the check—these logical decisions are not viewed through a logical lens. Instead, they are felt, they create hurt, they are fought.

That's when supervisors learn that their job is not just about leading. It's not just about being supportive. It's also about hard decisions and uncomfortable conversations. It means calling people on their stuff. It means...conflict. It means not being liked. It often means being the bad guy.

And who in the world joins a nonprofit to be the bad guy?

The Supervisor's Role

So if it's not about being liked, it's not about being the buddy, what *is* the job of supervisors and how they relate to their staff members?

I can break it down into the four major roles:
1. Set goals.
2. Support the staff.
3. Reward them.
4. Hold them accountable.

The nonprofit supervisor tends to focus on numbers 2 and 3, supporting and rewarding. Why? Because that's the fun stuff!

When we get to sit with our staff and support them, we get to be the good guy. We ask them how it's going, we offer sage advice, we identify what they need, and then we help them get it. We are the heroes!

We also love to reward. We tell our staff what a great job they did on something. We announce our department's successes in front of everyone else at a full staff meeting, and we just know that they all wish they could report to *us* instead of to their own bosses.

Sarcasm aside, I do recognize that these are important steps, and you'll spend a whole lot of time on these as a supervisor. And you should.

But...

Do not skip steps 1 and 4, even though as supervisors we are all tempted to do so.

Why the temptation? Why don't we set goals? Why don't we hold our staff accountable? Read on.

Why we avoid Step 1: Setting Goals

Truth be told, often we simply don't think about it. When we first fill a position, we are so busy and so glad to get staff in the door doing the work that we don't start out with the big picture. We just want to get them going immediately. We figure they got the job because they read the description, interviewed for it, and asked us lots of questions. We figure this is good enough to get them started.

We also don't always talk about the organizational and department goals to our staff because sometimes even we don't know what they are. Perhaps they've never even been created. And so we go back to the job description, which includes a list of activities, but not the goals—not what the person needs to achieve this year, this month, or this week. Not things like money raised, clients engaged, marketing materials created, or new IT servers researched.

Make sure your staff knows the big picture: the mission, the goals/strategies of your strategic plan, and the part they play in getting you there.

Know this: If you fail to do step 1, if you do not have that initial conversation with your staff members that outlines the goals they should be striving for and the steps they should take on a daily basis to get there, you are setting your staff members up to fail.

You are also leaving your organization—and the fulfillment of your mission—up to chance. That's not good enough. Your staff is expensive. It's up to you to make sure they are being used strategically, effectively, and wisely.

What if *you* don't know the goals you're supposed to be reaching? Get your boss, your board—whoever should know—to tell you. And if they don't know, create them.

Then pass it on.

Why we avoid Step 4: Accountability

Most of us hate holding our staff members accountable, especially when it means having a hard conversation.

- We don't get into this work to tell our staff the uncomfortable news that they're not performing the way we need them to.
- We don't think about our professional lives and dream of the day we get to give our staff a bad evaluation.
- We don't envision addressing the subjective stuff—the stuff that is messy and personal, such as inappropriate dress, lack of organizational skill, and emails riddled with grammatical errors.

Yet we become supervisors and all of a sudden these issues pop up, and it's up to us to address them.

And those of us who are doing our jobs get it done. Yet far, far more of us do not. Why?

- Because it's uncomfortable.
- Because it's personal.
- Because, chances are, we won't be liked very much once it's over.

As you find yourself squirming at the thought of conflict and talking yourself out of a hard conversation, know this: Managers sell their staff short if they don't do step 4. Nobody is perfect. We all have room to grow. Everyone needs critical feedback to do the job better. Your organization deserves it.

And it's your job.

HARD CONVERSATIONS: HOW TO HAVE THEM

Yes, hard conversations with staff are tough. Conflict is hard. And, frankly, not being liked as a result stinks. But none of that is an excuse not to hold these conversations.

So how do you do it right?

Here are some tips:

- Tip 1: Do supervision steps 1 through 3 to put yourself in a decent starting place. Your staff should know what their goals are, and you should have supported them and rewarded them for those things that exceeded expectations in some way. This is part of the comprehensive job of being a good supervisor. Plus, if they know their goals, they know how they're measuring up (or not) and the hard conversation makes more sense. It's also a lot more fair.

- Tip 2: Do step 4 thoughtfully, with carefully chosen words. You should not do this on the fly, or as part of a different, casual conversation. Schedule a separate meeting to discuss this and this alone, and know that it can be brief. This isn't point/counterpoint. This is you letting your staff member know that you have concerns, and what you expect the person to do about it.

- Tip 3: Schedule it soon, in the day you know about the problem. As a supervisor, your gut will tell you when a seemingly innocent incident has become a pattern or turned into a bigger personnel concern. Once you figure it out, schedule a meeting to discuss it as soon as possible. It's too easy to talk yourself out of the conversation otherwise. I also made sure I scheduled these meetings first thing, just to get them off my plate and out of my head.

- Tip 4: Think ahead of time, but don't be so scripted that you can't respond to the conversation in the moment. Be clear on your main points and make sure they come across.

- Tip 5: Use "I" and "we" statements. For example, "As we discussed, this position requires XXX. I am having some concerns about your performance in this area. I need to see XXX." Don't point your finger at the person and say things like "you've really messed up here." That makes it personal (see next point).

- Tip 6: Don't let the conversation get personal, even if the matter itself is personal. If the staff member is chronically late, keep it to the matter at hand: "It is critical that you be punctual. I understand this has not been the case. I need you to address this issue and arrive on time regularly." It will be tempting for the staff member to get into all of the personal reasons why he or she is late. In the end, it doesn't matter. You can be kind and compassionate, but the fact is the person needs to change a behavior. Address the problem, clarify your expectations, and give the person ample opportunity to improve.

- Tip 7: Discuss the concern; don't debate the example. There's a difference between a concern and an *example* of that concern. When a person is chronically late for meetings, that is a personnel issue. When you cite the last time it happened, that's an example. Examples help you illustrate your point, but if you focus only on them you'll spend all kinds of time hearing the reasons behind each and every one.. This is not the point. The point is that the staff member is chronically late, and you know it. You trust yourself to be fair and to address only issues you know are true. If you find yourself backtracking, or if the conversation is going on too long, it probably means the person is getting to you. The staff member is debating a certain instance or accusing you of being rash. You're not. You've recognized a pattern and you know this is an issue—even if you haven't witnessed it all firsthand each time.

- Tip 8: Show that you take the problem seriously and tell the staff member how you will follow up. If it's serious enough, you want to give a date when you will meet to reevaluate. Set the meeting now, while you're feeling strong, not later, when the issue appears to have gone away and the staff member has told you a great joke that's gotten you laughing that week. If the situation is important enough, put it in writing, ending with some ideas about consequences, and including that it might lead to termination. (Check with your HR professional on the final draft, of course.) This is hard stuff to say, so I always made sure it was in writing in case I got cold feet. I then had the person read the write-up while we sat there.

I've had to hold these hard conversations more times than I can count and in a number of different organizations. I hated each one.

But I also knew my organizations were relying on me to ensure every single resource was being used effectively and efficiently, and the people were the most expensive of the bunch. Was I reasonable with my staff? Absolutely. Did I know that things happen? For sure.

But when patterns arose or I felt in my gut that I was letting a bad behavior go on, I had no choice but to meet it head on. Staff didn't always respond professionally. Sometimes they cried. And sometimes they left my office and talked about me to their peers.

And even though it stung, I knew this was part of being a supervisor; sometimes you have to be the bad guy. Which is why your job is lonely. (See page 150.) Which is why you cannot rely on your staff to be on your SWAT team. (See page 151.)

A final word on Step 4

Don't wait for a staff member's evaluation to bring up a concern. (See page 85.) That's not fair to the person and it's not good for the organization. Address performance or behavior issues immediately, and if you've already discussed a problem and it happens again, follow up. Once you've done the hard work by introducing the topic, you then need to show you're serious.

The Fifth Role: Adapting

The four roles are pretty solid. They are objective, and I can't find an argument against any of them. But there's a fifth role every supervisor must face, and it's somewhat messy.

Within the parameters of the four roles—and remembering that life is about politics and feelings as much as policies and fact—you also need to adapt to the various styles of your staff members.

And make no mistake—their styles will be different. All of them.

While we are all individuals working together toward a common purpose, that individuality means we all come to our work with different experiences, learning styles, values, priorities, and levels of self-confidence.

Individuality is a wonderful thing. We can all learn from each other and stimulate each other in new ways. At the same time, as supervisors, this requires us to manage each person differently—within the same parameters and based on the same goals and policies, yes, but differently within them.

Because in the end we are all different. Here are some examples:

- Some people are analytical thinkers and need significant time to think things through before diving into a project. Some are driven with an eye only for the outcome, and tend to dive in head-first without thinking about the process that will get them there.
- Some people need lots of validation. Some are completely independent.
- Some are overly confident. Some suffer from a horrible lack of self-esteem.

None of these characteristics is right or wrong. They are all different. And as a supervisor you need to know the various traits of your staff members, how to keep them motivated, how to reward them, and how to provide feedback in a way they will hear it. You need to adapt your meetings and your discussions to their needs. You need to set them—and your organization—up for success.

How do you do this? By getting to know them. By having regularly scheduled meetings—both individually and as a group. By staying professional, but also knowing the circumstances they bring with them to the job. Are they single or married? Do they have children? Are they financially secure? Do they spend each evening knitting or clubbing or playing poker?

Pay attention to how they respond to you when you meet, how they manage their workloads, how they communicate with others.

Get to know what makes them tick and how to best tell them that they need to stop wearing tank tops to work. This isn't about whether or not you should enforce the rules or implement the supervision steps. This is about how you will do so most effectively.

Supervision requires some intuition—which means knowing your staff and using the right words at the right time to ensure the organization is getting what it needs out of them, and that you are, too.

LEARN FROM ME: HOW I MESSED UP MY FIRST SUPERVISION JOB AND HOW I GOT BETTER

When I got my very first job as a supervisor, I was delighted. I'd moved up the ranks within my company and was now heading up my department (which, as a side note, brings with it its very own set of very messy challenges).

So I was now the boss of my former peers and had existing personal relationships with some of them. I was excited because I was now their supervisor. They were excited because they thought life was going to be easy.

At the time I had three staff members, who together provide a perfect picture of the various challenges facing supervisors.

Employee 1: Cindy

Cindy took my old position in the department. She was new, and offered my one opportunity to supervise someone who hadn't known me before I was the boss of the department. She was diligent and hard-working. She was also more than a little intense.

I'll be honest—she scared me.

When things were working and projects were flying, we were great together. But when I needed to address an issue or we didn't agree, she was quiet and cold. She didn't look me in the eye and she pursed her lips, clearly frustrated but not expressing it in words. It made things uncomfortable for the entire department. It made us less effective as a team.

I should have called her on the problem. I should have explored it. I should have validated her feelings, but also set expectations about her behavior. I should have made sure we were functioning well so that our department could get things done. I should have confidently supervised her and figured out what the issues were so she could feel good about being a part of the team.

I didn't.

Instead we functioned together awkwardly, and the work suffered as a result. She did what she wanted and I let her, even when it wasn't the best strategy. Our department wasn't as good as it could have been. And it was my fault.

Employee 2: Gina

Gina was our writer. She and I were friends before I became her boss.

Gina was smart. She knew that I was trying hard to be good at being the boss, and she...well... kissed my butt. At the time I was pleased to be validated in my position, and so I didn't set boundaries when she continued to confide in me as a friend. Our supervision sessions lasted more than two hours, with a lot of focus on her personal life. Meanwhile, issues that arose about her performance went unaddressed. Other staff—the ones she was supposed to be serving through excellent copywriting of their programs—became frustrated. Our department wasn't as good as it could have been. And it was my fault.

Employee 3: Lila

Lila had been our receptionist only a short time when I stepped into my new role. She was someone I cared for as a friend, someone who confided in me and someone I'd tried to help sort through some personal issues before I became her boss. In a way this was similar to my situation with Gina, but it turned out to present a whole different challenge.

That's because, when our budget took a hit and we had to cut staff, Lila turned out to be one of the victims. And it was up to me to tell her.

It turns out that we made the decision to cut Lila while she was on leave recovering from minor surgery. The day I was to drive to her house to lay her off, I lost my nerve.

I was sick to my stomach and called hubby crying, saying I couldn't do it. In the end I had to bring the HR person along with me to do the deed. It was a moment of weakness, a moment when I let a personal relationship get in the way of what I needed to do as a supervisor. It was a time when I did not reflect the strength—or the grace—of what it means to manage people. It made a difficult situation even worse. And it was my fault.

Lessons Learned

How did I get better at supervision? By learning from each mistake. By figuring out the four roles of supervision and sticking to them, then by adapting to the characteristics within them. By understanding that in the end, we are all in it for the mission—and that it was my obligation to keep that as my first priority. By acknowledging that people weren't going to like me all the time. By getting a good team of people on the outside to support me and tell me that I was still a good person.

Most importantly, I forced myself to have those hard conversations and saw that I survived them—and that the organization benefited as a result.

This bears repeating: Supervising can be incredibly rewarding. But when it's done right, it's also very hard. Just know this fact going in, and commit to it anyway (or get out of the way).

Here's the other thing you need to know.

Having the title of supervisor does not by definition garner respect for you or your work. Your title means that your staff members need to listen to you and do what you say. It does not mean they will respect you. It does not mean they should.

You need to do your part. You need to show them that you understand their role, its challenges and its nuances. You need to be fair and consistent in the way you work with them. You need to set up clear expectations and meet with them on a regular basis, providing good and critical feedback throughout the process.

You cannot be their friend, but you cannot treat them like a cog in a machine, either.

No matter what, in the end they might not like you. And, frankly, sometimes that means you're doing it right.

Chapter 11

EVALUATING YOUR STAFF

First, the big misconception.

When we think about the best way to address performance issues with our staff, many of us look to the most obvious, and perhaps best-named, document for this purpose: the evaluation.

Let me say that I'm a huge proponent of regular, consistent, and intentional evaluations. They are a built-in way of assuring you are working with staff members to recognize their strengths, identify their opportunities for improvement, discuss their goals for the coming year, and provide a space for real, one-on-one discussion about each staff member's performance and supervisory needs.

But . . .

The evaluation tool is just that…a *tool* for dialogue. Yet so often it is used as the dialogue itself. I've seen managers focus on the good stuff only, thinking this is a nice way to reward people—in writing—for their hard work. I've also seen supervisors use it to replace the real dialogue that needed to happen around performance issues all year long. There's also the evaluation sheet that is all scales and numbers, allowing you to quickly circle 5 out of 5 on everything, hand it over to HR, and move on to your next thing.

These are all lost opportunities, and bad for the organization.

The evaluation document must be created so that it clearly outlines the goals that have already been set, measures performance based on those goals, and also explores more subjective areas like communication, organization, professionalism, and meeting of deadlines.

I prefer evaluations that include open-ended questions, forcing the supervisor to write up a paragraph or two on a variety of performance measures. The important thing is to know that the document should *supplement* the dialogue you have with your staff members about their performance. It should be the way you record your kudos and concerns, and it should be your mechanism that allows each staff member to reflect later on what you've discussed in person.

Now that I've said this, I can also tell you something else.

I hated it when evaluation time came around. I hated it for the exact reasons so many supervisors do. I knew that it was going to force some difficult conversations. I knew it was going to be uncomfortable. I knew I would most likely see some tears. Yet I also knew evaluations were incredibly important, and that the reason they made me so uncomfortable was that there were some issues to be addressed.

I hated it, but I did the evaluations anyway. And I learned, and I got better at them.

Now, some tips on using the evaluation to get the best results for your organization.

Tip 1. Take it seriously.

Evaluations are not simply one more thing to tick off of your to-do list. They should not be done quickly or without a good amount of thought. Set aside some time, think through the questions before you begin, consider the goals and the staff member's performance toward them, think through the person's more subjective skills, and very intentionally write out the good and the bad. Choose your words carefully. Be direct. Don't make it personal. Do this ahead of time so you can sit with your thoughts, review the document another time, and see if you got it right.

Tip 2. Do it in your office.

The evaluation is a time to show you are the boss. The staff members need to come to your work space, and you need to sit across from them and look them in the eye. Walk them through the evaluation piece by piece so they don't just skip ahead to the juicy parts. Make sure you honor all of the good stuff, because you will also, carefully, include the issues that need to be addressed.

Tip 3. Have staff members evaluate themselves beforehand.

We had a self-evaluation form that paralleled the evaluation tool, and we required staff members to give it to the supervisor ahead of time. This was extremely helpful because it gave me a sense of what they believed to be their focus areas. It also illustrated their level of introspection, where our perspectives aligned with and contradicted each other, and what might surprise them during our discussion. Which leads me to my next tip, about surprises during evaluations.

Tip 4. No surprises!

There really shouldn't be any.

As I mentioned at the top, far too often supervisors use the evaluation as *the review for the whole year,* the one and only time when you explore both strengths and, even more so, weaknesses.

Do not put off difficult conversations with staff members because an evaluation is coming up. Nobody should ever hear about a performance concern for the first time during an evaluation. It is a sign of conflict avoidance on the supervisor's part, it's unfair, and it's a disservice to both the staff member and the organization because it means less-than-optimal performance has been allowed to continue.

Tip 5. Get a great tool and find a great process.

Some evaluation tools have rating scales and some have open-ended questions. Some evaluations occur on the staff member's anniversary and some organizations conduct them all at once. Most ask questions differently to get at performance successes and struggles. This tip is about getting your tool and finding your process—the ones that work best for your organization. There are plenty of great evaluation tools available that you can adapt. Don't go thinking that your organization is so nuanced that you need to create your own tool from scratch. Asking questions about your mission doesn't get at the real issues of performance *toward* that mission. This is about staff members' objective performance toward their goals, and their subjective behaviors as part of the team.

Tip 6. Make it worth their while.

Honoring staff—especially those who perform above expectations—is critical to your organization's success. Providing pay raises based on the outcome of the evaluation is a professional, respectful thing to do.

Too often nonprofits believe that a poverty mentality, which includes terrible salaries for all, is simply part of working in the sector. While we all know there are limits, I say your staff determines your organization's ability to meet its goals, to meet its mission. Compensation should be considered as a major factor in the nonprofit's overall sustainability. Do what you can to treat your star performers like star performers.

And while we'd all like to pretend that doing good work for the organization is enough to sustain staff energy each day, this is a fantasy. People need to be validated in all kinds of ways. That's why evaluations are important, because you're putting in writing the strengths that you've seen over the year. That's also why it's important to reward those strengths with some kind of financial benefit. It gives credence to all of your positive feedback, and also shows those who have not been performing that there is a tangible consequence to their shortcomings.

I took raises seriously. When I first stepped into the ED role, salaries had been frozen, so I thawed them. I made heavy budget cuts in order to bring pay increases back because I believed it was important to treat our professionals as professionals, and to treat our business like a business.

If you don't have money for a pay raise, you're not off the hook on an evaluation. Your staff still needs a formal way to hear from you how they are doing and what they need to work on.

As an alternative to raises, come up with other, creative ways to add benefit and validate the excellent performers. Let them attend a conference, give them an extra day off, or have a special breakfast for anybody who got to a certain level during the review. Do something to reflect your appreciation. Altruism is nice, but it's not the only thing that will keep your staff members working hard for you.

Then do everything you can to include pay increases next year.

Chapter 12

RECRUITING YOUR STAFF

Recruitment is not just something you need to get done when someone tells you he or she is leaving and you have a new space to fill.

It is an opportunity. No matter who is leaving, no matter how great that person might be, filling a role in your organization is your chance to bring in both new talent to meet your emerging needs and a dose of fresh energy.

Recruitment is also *the* most important thing you do.

Your staff is your greatest, most expensive resource. Getting the right people to work for you will make or break your organization, as well as your day-to-day professional life.

Recruit the right person (and do all the things listed in the supervision section; see page 70) and you're off to a great start. Recruit the wrong person—and it happens often—and you'll spend a whole lot of time redefining roles and realigning work and re-explaining why you need to do so.

Of course, as a manager you, by nature, spend a whole lot of time working with your staff members. But that time should be about reaching organizational goals, supporting your staff in doing so, and helping them course correct along the way. It should not be about performance improvement plans, a string of uncomfortable conversations, and calls to HR to figure out how to avoid unnecessary liability. It's a drain for all involved, and it makes everyone miserable.

Avoid this by spending the time and doing the work to get the right person in the door.

Or at least try, and know that sometimes even when you do, it just won't work out.

A wonderful HR professional once told me that every hire is about a 50/50 crapshoot, and frankly that's about my record.

Recruiting Well

How can you better your odds? Here are a few tips:

Tip 1. Recruit carefully.
Take the time and take it seriously. Understand how important this is to you and to your organization. Think it through. Do not blow this off. (Am I getting my message across?)

Tip 2. Write a great job description.
Create a document with absolute focus on the goals of the position and what you need. Use an open position to rethink how you might define it differently to meet the emerging needs of your organization.

Tip 3. Narrow down by phone.
After going through résumés and picking my top candidates, I always began with a phone call. The conversation got at some of my initial questions about their experience and their style, and also gave me the chance to tell the person the salary range. Often, I'd know within the first few minutes whether or not the candidate was appropriate for the next round. It saved us both a lot of time.

Tip 4. Have a panel.
I often asked other staff members to join me in the interviews. While they knew I'd make the final decision, their involvement provided additional feedback as I considered the candidates, while also giving me a sense of how the candidates would engage with them.

Tip 5. Ask pointed questions.

Ask excellent and direct interview questions. Include some traditional favorites that get at the candidates' history and work style. Ask about their communication techniques and how they meet deadlines. Ask what success means to them. Ask about their favorite boss. Further narrow down your favorites and consider a second round of interviews. As you do so, begin to ask more scenario-type questions that get at real situations they might encounter on the job. Pay attention to the questions they ask you to see if they've done their homework on your organization, and to get a sense of how seriously they want this particular job with your particular organization.

Tip 6. Be a tough reference checker.

When you've got your finalists, request a good set of references. I often asked for a former supervisor, as well as someone the candidate supervised. I began with the list, but was also known to use that as a starting point and check in with others at the candidate's former organizations. I was a tough questioner and got as much from each reference as I could.

Tip 7. Don't settle.

Don't make a decision because you simply need to get the process done or because you're drowning due to the fact that the position is open. A rash decision will come back to haunt you later. Have a dialogue with your finalists—perhaps away from the interview committee and the office, to see if their communication and professional styles will work with yours. In the end, if you haven't found the right person, acknowledge it and start over. It's better to have a position empty and to keep looking than to hire the wrong person and deal with the drama it creates later.

Tip 8. Avoid the Mission Myth.

This one might surprise you. Take special note and be a bit wary if a candidate is *too* connected to your mission. Consider whether the person's passion is so great that it could lead to boundary issues. While you want staff members to care about your organization, you also need them to function within your machine, and to understand that hard decisions will need to be made in the future. Ask these individuals to identify how they would be able to make tough management decisions, such as programmatic or staff cuts.

Tip 9. Don't fall for the big lie.

One thing I found very important in staff performance was the ability to be and stay organized. The nonprofit world is a busy place, and people need to be able to juggle. A lot. I always included a question about organization as part of the interview and—after falling for it on more than one occasion—came to realize that there is one answer that is never, ever true. At least not in my experience. Be wary if the response is the following, or something like it:

"My desk is a mess. But the funny thing is I know where everything is. People don't believe it, but I can find anything I need in a matter of seconds."

It's a lie. I'm not saying it's an intentional lie because some people really do believe they have this gift. But when it comes time to prove it they simply can't deliver. From everything I've seen, people with messy desks just aren't organized enough to know where everything is amidst the piles of paper. If they were, there would be no piles.

Tip 10: Don't oversell.

I learned this one the way I learned most of my lessons—through pain. It used to be that I treated strong candidates the way I treated donors—by giving a sales pitch. This was especially true when I was working to raise a position to a new level, bringing in a new set of experience, skill, and leadership. I aimed high when I recruited, and it often worked out great.

It didn't, however, when I tried to sway people to work for us who weren't necessarily excited about our organization or our pay rate. I somehow thought if I could just convince these people, they'd see in time that this was the perfect job for them. When they brought up concerns about the work or the nonprofit culture, or hedged at the pay, I'd talk to them about what a tremendous experience it was to work for our organization. I told them that I needed a partner in this game. I told them they wouldn't be sorry.

I oversold. Because sometimes it wasn't a pleasure at all to work for our organization or to be on my team. Sometimes it was hard, hard work. And, especially in those first few years of transition to a more business-minded culture, it was frustrating. These people, the ones I convinced, never lasted.

Recruiting means finding the person who is invested in your organization and in being successful at his or her job. It means finding someone with the skill, style, flexibility, and professionalism to take on the job—no matter what the circumstances. It means finding someone who can hear the truth about every part of the organization and wants the job anyway.

LEARN FROM ME: HOW I HIRED THE WRONG PERSON AND PAID THE PRICE

I bring you the story of Sara.

Sara interviewed for the job of finance director because she was tired of her current job. She needed to make a change, she said. She thought it was time to mix things up, she said. She thought it would be fun, she said. And I nodded and told her she should and told her it would.

Yet deep down I knew this wasn't the truth at all. The truth was we had just ended a difficult fiscal year and the books needed to be redone from scratch. We didn't have a budget. We had an audit coming up, a board that hadn't gotten financials in months, and a finance committee that was getting understandably antsy about it all.

The day she accepted the position was a day of pride for me. I had swung her to our side. She would be great. She would...save me. She lasted less than a month.

It came to an end on a Friday. I'd had a fantastic coffee meeting with a board member and returned to the office just to gather up my belongings and go home for the weekend, basking in all of the wonderful things I'd done to help the organization.

It was 4:45. Just one last check of emails before my celebration could begin, and...

There it was—an email from Sara. The subject line read: *Now for the really bad news.*

I closed my eyes for a second and caught my breath. I didn't even need to read it.

It said that she had decided to leave CAP. It said that she didn't have a true understanding about what she was walking into when she first accepted the job. It said that her old boss had wooed her back.

I tried to do the same. But this time my convincing, my pitch, didn't work.

In the end she said simply: "Life is too short, you know?" And I did know. I also knew it was my fault. I hadn't been clear. I hadn't been articulate. I hadn't been *honest.*

Chapter 13

SUCCESSION

Now that you've recruited the right team, you're set for the time being. Congratulations!

But, as you probably suspect, you can't stop now. Because you need to make sure your team is just as strong in the future. Which means you need to think about succession.

Succession seems to be a dirty word for many. That's because people take it personally.

Yet it's not a personal thing. Not even when it's about replacing you.

Nonprofit boards and leaders must engage in succession planning. This means thinking ahead to a time when the executive director and other staff are no longer a part of the organization. It means planning how you will get what you need for the organization once they are gone, and the process that will ensure their replacements have the experience and skills to get the work done at the organization—and perhaps even elevate it in some way.

It gets personal because this insinuates that the people currently in the seats *haven't* elevated it, and perhaps don't have the skills and experience to manage the organization and its needs.

This, of course, is silly.

Succession planning is about a position in the organization, not the person in it at the moment. It is not only a good practice but a *best* practice, and it means the staff and board are doing their obligatory work to ensure the organization is sustained into the future, no matter who is in the seats.

Make no mistake about it: Nobody is indispensable. Not your founder or you. Not your board chair or your longtime development coordinator. If an organization has healthy and functional systems in place, then the people in and out of the seats cannot make or break the organization. They may be missed mightily, but their absence won't sink anything.

Let's face it: If we're really being honest with ourselves, many of us would prefer to think that an organization could never survive quite so well without our unique skills, charms, and expertise. Yet we know deep down that the prospect of any one person having so much power that his or her absence would kill an organization is just bad business. The focus shifts from what's best for the mission to what's best for the person and how to keep that person happy.

And if it is even remotely true—that one person has so many contacts, and so much knowledge that is not transferable—then you need to fix it. The person could be recruited away, could win the lottery, and, yes, could get hit by that proverbial bus. Why would you allow that kind of liability to exist when you care so deeply about your organization?

Embrace succession planning, even though it might hurt some feelings. Be clear that this is about planning for the organization's future, not about getting people out of their current seats.

Succession Planning: How to Do It

Now that we've got all of those hurt feelings out of the way, what does succession planning really mean?

It means asking thoughtful questions about key positions:

- When a certain position is vacant, who will immediately fill those needs?
- How will you determine the best way to recruit for it?
- Who will you pull in for the discussion?
- In the case of the executive director, are there firms or companies that can help find an interim person?
- Is there a reason to consider a current staff member to fill

that role? (I've found this to be a tricky option.) Is there a reason for a board member to fill that role? (Even trickier!)

- Do you have a sense of everything each position does? Are the job descriptions up to date? Do you want to use this as an opportunity to restructure things somehow?
- What will your recruiting process be? Are there any obvious candidates for the position? Is the pay currently what it needs to be or should it be adjusted?

Succession planning is another part of a good system. It's about a process, not specific personnel. As a leader you need to make that clear, move on, and do what's right for the organization.

Chapter 14

DELEGATION

For some of us, delegation is a very natural thing. There is nothing that pleases us more than determining which tasks are appropriate for which people, and then moving them off our proverbial plate and onto another's.

For others, delegation is a foreign concept. This is especially true for nonprofit leaders, who often don't have the luxury of extra positions and large staff sizes, whose staff is already taking on more than their job descriptions entail, who work extra-long hours for very little money, and who find themselves on the fast track to burnout.

Throw in that many nonprofit leaders tend to just want to get stuff done, and delegation doesn't even enter their minds.

I say it should.

Why? Because your organization will works most efficiently when it does.

Far too often nonprofits happily engage in the clubhouse effect, the "all for one and one for all" mentality, when we all pitch in to get a job done. And sometimes that's exactly what needs to happen in the short term.

But…

That's the exception. The rest of the time you need the right people in the right positions utilizing the right skills to meet the diverse needs of the organization.

LEARN FROM ME: HOW I TRIED TO DO IT ALL AND REALIZED THAT MAKES IT WORSE

Though I had a staff of 40 at my organization, each person was tasked with his or her own specific outcomes, along with all kinds of other duties that kept our nonprofit going strong—things like attending our fundraising events, emptying our kitchen dishwasher, and assisting with mailings.

When I first took the job, I found myself engaging in tasks that made absolutely no sense in my role—not just because I was the ED, but because it was silly for the organization to pay me my hourly rate so that I could pick out new paint colors or restock the office supply cabinet.

My moment of clarity came the day I returned to the office from a meeting only to find that we had a leak in the bathroom, the copy machine was broken, and the server was down. Staff members were waiting outside my door in a panic, looking to me for help. Why? Because until that day I had taken care of such things. I got them done. I didn't even think about asking other staff to take on extra tasks because, I rationalized, they had their own items to get done.

But that day, as I thought about who to call first—our landlord, our IT guy, or our copy maintenance guy—I actually froze with the phone piece halfway to my ear.

And then I just knew. This was stupid.

If we were going to truly run like a business, I needed to think about things differently. And so I decided to create an administrative position to handle all of these kinds of issues.

Did I have the funds? No, but I was creative. I found a position that was more of a part-time job, expanded the hours a bit and integrated some administrative needs into it. The next budget year, I built in a full-time position for these kinds of tasks and moved funding around to make it happen. I didn't let myself feel guilty about it. This was best for the organization, one more step toward getting the machine working optimally.

Chapter 15

VOLUNTEERS

Volunteers play a critical role in many organizations, especially those that are new or small, the ones that don't yet have the resources to bring on paid staff.

Because of their passion, their commitment, and their willingness to take on jobs of all shapes and sizes, volunteers can be found in just about every organization. You could certainly find them at mine.

I thought it would be an easy relationship. I thought this was something that just couldn't get messed up. And, as with everything else, it just wasn't that simple.

Our organization was evolving into a newly defined business, which meant our volunteer program needed to do the same. This proved to be a challenge, one that got personal and messy.

Over time we figured out how to overcome that challenge and better utilize our volunteers for the good of the organization. It wasn't easy, but we learned our lessons. And, just like so many others, those lessons came only after doing things wrong the first time.

The Mistakes We Made with Our Volunteers and How We Fixed Them

Mistake 1: We didn't treat them right.
Notice that I did not say we didn't treat them *well*. I think it's safe to say we did. But we didn't work with them effectively, or think about them the right way.

When I first interacted with our volunteers, I did so in a way that was very similar to the way I interacted with our clients. I had this idea that we were serving our volunteers, that they were natural beneficiaries of our organization.

This led to the sense that our volunteers were untouchable. It meant that they could arrive in our offices and expect to be served in whatever way they desired. It meant that they could focus on getting their needs met, and that our job was to make it happen.

Don't get me wrong: Volunteers are generous people. They contribute something valuable to the organization and must be treated well. But in the end, their work must serve the organization first.

Once I realized this, I stopped thinking about volunteers as clients and began thinking about them as unpaid staff. Which meant we needed to treat them as such, engaging them in a different way, focusing on the four roles of supervision. (See page 72.) We needed to recruit them into roles that matched their skills, and we needed to let them know what we expected from them in return.

Expected, you ask? Isn't that a harsh word for a volunteer role? No. Remember, human resources are the most important asset at an organization. They make or break how the work gets done—oftentimes, whether the mission is fulfilled at all.

After making the expectations clear, we then supported our volunteers in achieving their goals, rewarding them for their successes and holding them accountable when issues arose.

Wait a second, you ask. *You held them accountable?*

Yes. When there were issues with performance or behavioral concerns, we needed to have those difficult conversations, the same kind we had with staff. (See page 74.) We were kind, and we honored the fact that they were donating their time, but we also told them what was no longer acceptable. And sometimes, no matter how hard we tried to make it work, the volunteer needed to be...

Fired.

Yes. It didn't happen often. In fact, let me pause to say that our volunteers were some of the most inspirational, passionate, committed people I have had the pleasure to meet. But, as with paid staff, some were not the right fit. And in those situations we began to do what we did with paid staff—hold the uncomfortable conversations, issue the warnings, and sometimes, terminate the partnership.

It happened just a few times, but when it did…oh, how things hit the proverbial fan!

On more than one occasion my board received angry letters from our volunteers, letters about how we'd treated them terribly. It was absolutely unheard of, they said. It was completely unfair, they said. It was a terrible way to treat the people who gave to our cause, they said.

Luckily, most of these letters came after the board and I had developed some trust. They knew that we were all there to make sure our goals were met efficiently and effectively, that it was our job to hold everyone to the highest of standards. They knew that we needed to be just, fair, and kind, but in the end we needed to get the work done.

Mistake 2: We gave them silly volunteer jobs.
It's a rare nonprofit that has all of the staff it truly needs to get the work done well. Volunteers are a great way to supplement these duties.

Utilizing volunteers to best meet the organization's needs means someone must plan ahead, identifying the various ways volunteers can truly provide a needed service, and figuring out how to find the best fit for each role.

But…

Far too often—and I've been guilty of this plenty—we don't do this. And it not only turns into a less-than-meaningful experience for the volunteer, but it is a wasted resource for the organization— one that could have helped the organization achieve its goals.

What winds up happening is that when the volunteers show up at the start of the day, those in charge of managing them have this uncomfortable moment of dread. There are no projects planned, and all of a sudden this asset of a few extra pairs of hands is one more thing to figure out, explain, and monitor. And we're overwhelmed, and we don't have the time.

And so we find some kind of menial task for the volunteers instead. We put them to work on projects that neither utilize their skills nor move the organization forward. At CAP, our volunteer crutch was the folding of red AIDS ribbons. Whenever we had volunteers come in—some of them incredibly skilled and motivated—and we hadn't planned ahead, we'd pull out the rolls of red ribbon and the pins and tell them to go to town.

I cringe when I think about how many thousands of red ribbons were created by accountants and fundraisers and administrative people—individuals who could have given so much to us. Individuals who wanted to make a real contribution. But we didn't plan. We didn't think through how to orient them to our much-needed tasks, and we were so busy with our own workloads that we wasted their skills.

In the end, we took on a more strategic plan, and we recruited volunteers to fit our needs. We designated one person on our staff to help coordinate the volunteer program. We also started doing something else when it came to new volunteers.

If they couldn't fill a need, we turned them down.

We finally realized the truth: that as we got bigger and added more staff, we really didn't have as many volunteer needs as we thought we did.

And that had to be okay, even though it was different from the way we'd worked historically, and even though the volunteers wanted to help us out. In the end, we realized that utilizing volunteers only when we had appropriate work to be done was better than spending time and energy managing volunteer projects that didn't benefit our mission. It was also better than bringing someone in who would then have a bad experience. You can't undo bad experiences.

Mistake 3: We didn't train them.

Once we identified the perfect volunteer task and the perfect volunteer fit, we then proceeded to make another mistake: We didn't tell them how to do it.

It happened because we were busy and overwhelmed, and we told ourselves it would be fine, that the work would get done. Yet we knew deep down that this was not only bad form, not only bad for the reputation of the organization, but it was also a potential liability.

We made this mistake in the worst way—with our front desk volunteers. We showed them their seats, then failed to explain to them how things worked, how to answer questions, or what we expected on a customer service level. And when they screwed up and we looked bad—which made our organization look bad—we had nobody to blame but ourselves.

Take the time to train your volunteers, to let them know what you expect from them. Conduct a general volunteer training/orientation at regular intervals to clarify general organizational policies and procedures.

Get your volunteers invested in you and they'll do a great job. Set them up for failure and everybody loses.

Mistake 4: We didn't keep them informed.

One thing I learned along the way—and it seems so obvious now— is that both staff and volunteers need to be informed.

Far too often I'd sit with my managers and we would update a policy or create a strategy, and then fail to let the staff in on it. The communications piece somehow went missing. And so our big new decisions meant nothing.

It took us a bit of time to figure out how to keep staff apprised of all changes. It took even longer to extend this notion to our volunteers.

So there they'd be, at the front desk, working in the food bank, helping out at an event, and someone would ask them a question about the organization. And they wouldn't know the answer, or, even worse, they'd get it wrong.

When you figure out all of the great new ways to communicate, you will create a better business for your nonprofit and get everyone in the loop—including those volunteers, who will bring those messages to everyone else.

And finally…

Mistake 5: We tripped all over the conflict-of-interest line.
Conflicts of interest are everywhere—often more so in the nonprofit sector than anywhere else. Board members get involved in competing organizations, staff members get romantic with their managers, clients want to be volunteers.

Dual relationships are not a bad thing, but they do need to be acknowledged, and strategies need to be in place so that they any potential conflicts can be addressed.

Ask the questions and think strategically about what you will do *before* a conflict happens. How would you feel about having a volunteer who also benefited from your services? What if the volunteer was related to a board member? How would you feel about a volunteer CPA who did the books for a competitor? How would you feel if your board member chaired the board of an organization that went after your very same donors?

If you decide these things aren't acceptable, get the policies in writing. Enforcing them won't be comfortable, but it's still easier than dealing with specific people in a specific situation and having to make a decision on the fly.

You also want to clearly state how boards will deal with conflicts and their voting rights. If a board member could benefit from a decision, it's common for that person to refrain from voting. For instance, if the board is taking a vote on a new auditing firm that happens to be the employer of a board member, that board member should recuse him- or herself from the vote.

Chapter 16

A FEW WORDS ON COMMITTEES

Like so many other things in nonprofit management, volunteer committees as a concept seem so simple and so…lovely. But often in practice they just…aren't.

The Mission Myth exists everywhere, which means people will care so deeply about your mission that they are willing to donate their time to your cause. That, in itself, is wonderful. Yet it's not just their expertise that comes to the table. It's also their accompanying, often strong, opinions.

Know this: Group dynamics and politics are *always* present. Just because committees have this air of altruistic purity about them does not mean you should execute them any less strategically than you do any other component of your organization.

Set up your committees for success from the beginning, and then adjust along the way.

And know that nothing is ever as easy as it seems.

Here are steps to creating a successful committee:

Step 1: Determine the goals.
It is pointless to create a committee, or to make any other effort, unless you know precisely why you're doing it. Committees are one more part or your machine. Make sure they're set up to achieve optimal results.

Create a committee because there's a project or ongoing initiative that needs outside perspective and assistance, because the organization needs a certain level of additional expertise, or because there aren't enough staff resources to get the job done.

The marketing team might require PR expertise to engage in media relations. A CFO needs an external means to provide checks and balances on the books. An art auction event requires...art, and people with connections to it. Committees could result from any of these needs.

And while these all justify the *existence* of a committee, they themselves are not enough to define what the committee will *do*. Will committee members actually carry out tasks or will they serve in an advisory capacity? Will they fill tables at the gala or determine the seating chart?

Define the goals and roles of committee members beforehand and be crystal clear about them as you recruit these members. Otherwise you're setting yourself up for plenty of assumptions, a growing level of frustration, and a good dose of hurt feelings in the end.

Step 2: Determine the type.

Some committees must be ongoing, or at least established as long-term bodies until a later date when they are up for evaluation (which you always want to do).

Others will be ad hoc, meaning they are formed specifically to tackle one task or project and will then disband. Examples are when an organization decides to redo its HR policies, create a board orientation strategy, or update the bylaws.

Ad hoc committees tend to be clear in their purpose from the beginning. Just make sure you define that purpose, the goals and objectives, the project timeline, and—this one is just as important—when and how you will know it is time to disband.

Step 3: Determine the context.

In addition to identifying whether this committee is ad hoc or ongoing, you want to think through whether this is a board committee or a volunteer committee.

Board committees exist to create or monitor a component that is relevant to the board's governance work. They are made up mostly of board members, though additional expertise might be brought to the table. Committee chairs tend to be board members, and often report regularly at board meetings. Examples of board committees are finance and audit committees.

Volunteer committees do not report to the board and instead communicate directly to the ED or another designated staff member. Reports about the goings-on of these committees may still be made at board meetings, but only because the board feels it needs updates.

An event committee is an example of a volunteer committee. We had an AIDS Walk Colorado committee at CAP, made up of representatives from several aspects of the event, including our corporate sponsors, our longtime volunteers, and, yes, a few board members. Its function was to advise the staff in decision making, ensuring that we were taking the various perspectives of our stakeholders into consideration as we planned for that year's event. Because it was our largest fundraising event and significantly impacted the budget, our staff reported to the board on the overall progress of the event. Yet the board didn't have official authority in running it.

Speaking of which...

Step 4: Determine the authority.
This step is big, but for some reason it's often ignored when committees are first formed. Big mistake.

You need to determine, and then state clearly, whether this committee will have the power to make decisions or will instead inform and advise others who have the power to do so.

The committee might get the final say on whether a press release is ready to go, or it might give advice on the wording but leave it to the staff or others to finalize the process. Figure this out ahead of time and name the committee appropriately. If it won't have the last word, you might want to add the word "advisory" to the title.

You also want to determine how decisions will be made, even if they are just for recommendation purposes. Will they be based on consensus or an outright vote? Will you need a quorum? Answer these questions ahead of time or set yourself up for some tension and conflict later on.

Step 5: Determine the staff role.

Chances are one or more staff members will—and should—sit on the committee. They not only bring an internal organizational perspective, but will most likely play some kind of role in carrying out the committee's recommendations or decisions in the future.

Decide up front what the role of these staff members will be. Are they strictly there to coordinate the logistics and handle the notes or administrative tasks related to this? Are they there to provide specific input? Are they leading the charge and asking for feedback from others so that they can then bring this information back to the staff or board?

Committees can be awkward for staff, especially if there are board members or donors involved. Set up the relationship and expectations ahead of time.

You also need to determine who will head up the committee. Who will facilitate and lead the discussion? How will the agenda for each meeting be set? Will there be formalized policies to follow, and if so, who will determine them? Will there be minutes after the meeting is over? Get all of these answers before the first meeting is even scheduled.

Step 6: Recruit carefully.

As with everything else, determining who you get on your team is the most important decision of all.

It is always tempting to go with convenience—bringing in those enthusiastic people who want to play a part without thinking about the fit.

Don't. Think through the skill sets and personality character-istics that will be most useful to the task at hand. Try to determine those who fit the bill and approach them directly. Then find others, and ask them questions that get at whether they will have the time, skills, and experience you need. Think ahead of time as to the ideal number on your committee and then strive for it. More is not neces-sarily better.

The great thing about committees is that they are fertile train-ing ground for board and staff members, which is why you always want your committee recruitment to be especially strategic.

Recruit carefully, being explicit about the goals of the commit-tee, the parameters you've determined, and the power this group will have. Train committee members and provide them with the information they need to get the job done. Orient them to the orga-nization and the task at hand. Respect their time, and expect that they will respect your organization in return.

Monitor along the way and address issues as they arise. And know that, just as with every other position, no committee post is guaranteed or expected to be permanent.

Chapter 17

CONSULTANTS

I went through a lot of consultants when I was an ED.

I use the words "went through" intentionally. While some of them worked well, met my needs, and were the right fit for my organization at the right time, some just weren't. And, to be fair, I wasn't the right fit for them either.

It makes sense that nonprofits engage with consultants. As with every other business, we all have specific skill sets, and we all need to fill in the gaps in order to ensure our organization has every resource it needs to run successfully.

The trick, of course, is finding the right person to fit your needs: someone who doesn't just possess the skills and expertise that you're looking for, but is also someone you can work with. Choose correctly and the consultant can make your life a lot easier. Choose incorrectly and you've got another personnel issue on your hands—and chances are you don't have the time, the energy, or the interest for it.

Like everything else, it's all about planning ahead.

How did I learn this? From pain, of course—from knowing that I needed someone to come in and balance my books and then winding up with a guy who spent his time tinkering with my chart of accounts. From bringing in someone to write grants who couldn't write. From hiring facilitators who were conflict avoidant. Chances are you've experienced something similar, or at least seen it. Which is why, in the end, many of us decide not to engage consultants at all. It just doesn't seem worth our time.

But…

I assure you it *is* worth your time, if it's done right. It doesn't just add a new level of skills and expertise to your organization. It also officially pinpoints a person who will get projects done for you—projects that you might otherwise have to do yourself, delegate to an already busy staff, or wind up crossing off the list when they really shouldn't be.

How to engage with the right consultant the right way?

Here are a couple of tips to help:

Tip 1. In general, think differently.
Many people engage in consulting relationships with one of a few preconceived notions.

First, they tend to think that because they're engaging someone who has a certain skill set they lack, they have no power in the relationship.

False.

They think that the consultant is just like a paid staff member, and so can be treated like one.

False.

They think the only real consideration when making a choice is expertise.

False.

They think that their nonprofit does such good work that the consultant should be willing to do the work for free or at a substantially reduced rate.

False. False. False.

Think of the consultant as a partner in achieving a specific goal or objective. This partnership is a professional one. This means that you need to select the consultant carefully, orient that person appropriately, define the parameters, communicate on an ongoing basis, and even transition the consultant out of the organization if the relationship is not working as expected.

You know more than you think you do about the topic of the consultant's expertise. After all, you know your organization's needs. If you feel intimidated because you're bringing in a skill set with which you are not familiar, you're not off the hook on finding the right fit. Ask colleagues who have engaged people in similar positions, and ask those you know who also have this expertise to help you figure out the questions to ask and what you should be looking for.

If you can at all help it, do not hire a consultant for free. You get what you pay for, and even if the person has the greatest skill set and the best of intentions, he or she needs to get paid by *somebody*. Which means your consultant then needs to take on paying clients, and chances are your project will fall to the bottom of the list. You also run the risk of being taken less seriously if the consultant feels you are getting a handout. All of a sudden that person goes from being a consultant to a donor, which is a different relationship. And all of a sudden you owe the consultant in a way you didn't before.

Tip 2: Get ready.

Where to begin when figuring out your partnership? With your goals, of course.

What exactly do you need? What are the goals of the short-term project or long-term services for which you will engage with the consultant? The clearer you are on what you need to get out of the relationship, the more you can explicitly state this to the person and hear how the consultant will meet those needs.

Create a brief job description that outlines any objectives or measures you need to see at the end, and include an estimated timeline. If you don't do this, the consultant will have to guess and will create the parameters for you.

Selecting a Consultant

As with staff, board, and key volunteer positions, start with those you know and trust. Go back to those colleagues who have needed a similar type of consultant and ask them for recommendations. Lessen your 50/50 odds of a successful hire (see page 89) by learning as much as you can about the specific individuals you might engage.

Which brings me to my next point about selection.

As with hiring a staff member, make sure you consider not just those hard, objective skills the person can bring to the organization, but also the subjective characteristics that will make or break this relationship for you.

What kind of communication style are you looking for? Do you want someone who flourishes independently, or do you want a detail-orientated communicator who will send an account of all his or her activities directly to your email inbox each day? How important is punctuality? Ability to articulate? Organization? We all know some consultants will be more personable than others. How important is that to you and to the project at hand?

Try to look at and consider more than one candidate, though if you've got a powerhouse, it's okay to look at just one—as long as you do your due diligence and don't hire too quickly because you're in a jam.

Engage in at least two discussions before anything is signed: one to explain what you need and one where the candidate comes back and tells you what he or she can do. Require that the candidate submit a proposal—complete with objectives, deliverables, timelines, and fees—and review it carefully to ensure the person understands what you need. Check references.

Every position is critical to the success of your organization, and engaging a consultant who doesn't perform is not only detrimental to your organization, it's also a royal pain for you. Who needs that?

Be careful about hiring consultants who are also board members, donors, volunteers, or clients, or someone closely related to any of these. It's a small world, yes, but you need to keep this relationship as professional as possible in order to get your needs met, get honest feedback on performance, and address concerns. If you do engage someone who has close ties to the organization, talk to this person about how you will keep the relationship at a professional level.

This is not a place to let personal feelings get in the way. I've seen it. I've lived it.

Working with One

Some consulting gigs will necessitate that the individual show up at your office each day. Such consultants are not paid staff, but there are some daily functions they will need to know in order to start things off right and to help them fit in. Will they need a key? A parking pass? A log-in to your computer system? Do you have a dress code at the office they need to be aware of?

Other projects will happen off-site, which means you need to determine ahead of time how you will check in with your consultant or, even better, how the consultant will check in with you. Do you need to talk daily? Weekly? Hourly?

No matter whether your consultant is internal or outside your organization, let staff know that this person will be a part of your team and why you brought the consultant on board, and then describe the specific function or goals of the relationship. You want them to know you've thought the decision through and carefully selected this person, and to help them support the relationship from the beginning.

Transitioning One Out

There are two reasons you will end a relationship with a consultant: The person either has completed the project or is not the fit you were hoping for.

Most often the transition will be the first type, and the way to do this as smoothly as possible is to clearly determine the deliverables and timelines of the project. Before it even starts, make sure you both understand how you'll know when it's over. It's very easy for both sides to get involved in what we refer to in the consultant world as "scope creep"—a CPA prepares your books for your audit, then winds up creating your financial statements that month. A consultant helps you achieve a fundraising plan, then you find yourselves talking about developing a new marketing brand.

Clearly lay out your expectations ahead of time, and don't expect additional work for nothing. If the project extends or continues into a new phase, be sure to communicate this and set up a new partnership, complete with a new scope of work and proposal.

If a consultant's transition is because he or she turns out to be the wrong fit, well, that's just a whole lot less fun. But it's equally as important to know and plan for, starting with clearly stating at the beginning and in writing that either partner can terminate at any time.

If you're not getting what you need and you don't feel you can get it, you must facilitate a transition. Consultants tend to be more expensive than staff, and continuing to pay one for services you aren't getting is bad for the organization. Handle the situation professionally, be direct, and don't let the person hang on for another few days or weeks if you can help it.

To be able to do this means you didn't let yourself get too personally involved in the relationship and you've kept appropriate boundaries. It can be tempting to engage a consultant as a confidant or colleague. Don't. Consultants need to know you are serious about this relationship and their performance.

Just one more reason the nonprofit executive job is so lonely. (See page 150.)

Chapter 18

CUSTOMER SERVICE

Why do donors and customers get involved with nonprofits?

Because they are passionate about—say it with me—the mission. Chances are that's what brings them to the nonprofit the first time.

Why do these same people come back?

Because they had a good experience the first time.

Being a nonprofit does not provide any kind of free pass on the way you treat your customers—and by customers, I mean each and every person who comes in contact with your organization. For any reason.

If you treat people well, they won't forget it. If you treat them poorly, if their call isn't returned or they're kept on hold for minutes at a time, if nobody thanks them for their support or they feel at all underappreciated, they won't forget that either. And the road to getting them back will be steep and difficult.

Think of your own experiences. What companies have treated you like gold? Did you feel special? Did you go back?

What companies treated you like a nobody or a number? Ignored you? Gave you attitude or chose to fight you on a minor issue that really didn't matter? Did you go back?

Providing good customer service means you won't just get customers involved in your organization one time; it means they'll come back. Which means you will have additional donations, board members who stay for a second term, and more clients who are getting their needs met.

It means your organization will run better and that you're doing good *well*.

It is critical that every single person related to your nonprofit understands this point. And it's up to nonprofit leaders to get these people on board, to set the expectation that excellence in this regard is the only option.

Leaders of nonprofits must also explain what excellence looks like. Be specific. Talk about who your customers are and how you expect them to be treated. Create policies and procedures about your expectations. For example...

- How quickly will you send out a letter thanking a donor for a gift? When do donors get a phone call as well?
- How will staff members answer their phones?
- How will staff address a customer when they walk by that person in the hallway?

Remember that the job's not done after you talk to staff about this. Make sure your volunteers are also made aware of your customer service expectations and policies, especially since they are often the ones interfacing with your stakeholders.

Common Customer Service Pitfalls

There are a few common ways customer service goes wrong. Here are some of them:

Pitfall 1: Reception malfunctions
You know this because you've lived it on the other side.

The reception area is your customers' introduction to how you go about your business. If they are greeted warmly—not just by those at the desk, but also by those who walk through the lobby—they feel valued. If they have to wait, if they are not acknowledged until they are staring a receptionist in the face, if they in any way feel they are a bother to any member of the organization, it will stick with them. And you might never see them again.

If there is a place to be extremely concrete in your customer service expectations, it's in your reception area. The individuals who staff this area interface with just about every stakeholder you have. Do not leave these interactions to chance. Be clear with your policies, recognize those who excel at customer service, and hold accountable those who don't.

Pitfall 2: Failure to follow through

It's a simple concept.

When you make commitments to customers, you must deliver. If you say you will call them or refer them to someone else, you cannot fail to do so. When you promise to get them a piece of information, get it to them, preferably before you said you would. If they call or email you, you must return the message.

It's a simple concept, but it's one we constantly let slip.

I understand. You are busy, and sometimes it just seems impossible to make the time to follow through. If that is truly, truly the case, then I say this: Don't commit in the first place. It's better not to promise anything than to promise something and not come through.

Pitfall 3: Failure to own a mistake

Customers and stakeholders will express their dissatisfaction in all kinds of ways. They'll tell you straight up. They'll email or call. They'll contact a board member.

Sometimes the issues they bring are valid. When this is the case, you need to own it. Apologize sincerely and let them know how you will remedy the situation.

Sometimes their issues feel just plain picky. They are without substance, related to a mundane detail. They can be irritating, especially if the individual making the complaint gets nasty or personal.

Do not let your irritation show in these moments. Whether or not your customers' problems are real to you, they are real to them. And they are your customers. They not only know about your organization, but they also have circles of colleagues who might hear about it from them. Handle the situation well, and your grace might not be acknowledged. Return their hostility and it'll be all over town.

So how do you handle this?

Do your best not to take these moments personally. Easy for me to say, yes. But trust me, I've been there. I've answered hundreds of phone calls/in-person complaints/emails from angry people who were not afraid to tell me why I was such a terrible person or my organization was subpar. I resisted the urge to fight back. I told them that I was sorry to hear they felt that way and I talked through how we might resolve the issue. There were plenty of times I did this through tightly gritted teeth, but for the most part they didn't know it.

One caveat on this point: Customer service does not mean you take abuse. When I found myself in situations where the other person got nasty, I kept my composure and said I needed to end the conversation. I told the person I would follow up at another time, when the situation calmed down. And I always did.

When mistakes happen or customers complain, handle it like a professional. You can kvetch about it later. We are only human, after all.

Pitfall 4: Forgetting to say thank you

It happens easily enough: With dozens, perhaps hundreds, of stakeholders wanting your attention, the rather benign "thank you" might fall away from your brain, preempted by your next to-do item. I urge you now—don't let this happen.

In fact, say the words "thank you" right now, as you read this.

It took you a second. It cost you nothing. If you do it by email, it might take a minute or two to get the message written. Yet the return can be exponential.

People like feeling valuable. There's nothing wrong with that. In fact, it gives us a pretty easy way to connect with them. Thanking people for their time, for their interest, for their efforts is one of the best ways to keep the warm feelings of connection between two individuals. That's what all of this is about, really. It's about connections—our connections to those we serve, our connections to those who give to us, our connections to the staff we work with each day. Even the biggest corporations are made up of thousands of individuals looking to make a connection. So make it, then seal it with a thank-you. They'll remember it—if not your words, then the warm sense of mutual respect they had after your meeting ended. Thank people for the smallest ways they extend themselves. It costs so little. It means so much.

And why wouldn't you? Why wouldn't you thank a donor and up your odds that he or she will give again? Why wouldn't you thank a staff member for going above and beyond what is expected, even in some small way?

Just be sure you are being authentic. You're not thanking someone just for showing up at the office that day. You're not thanking a low performer when that person decides to stick through to 5 p.m. instead of sneaking out early. Make sure there's a reason to show your gratitude, even if it's a small one. Make it genuine. Make it sincere. Make it a habit.

Pitfall 5: A messy office

Sometimes—oftentimes—the nonprofit office isn't exactly a royal kind of pad. The building itself might be run-down, it might not be in the safest of neighborhoods, it might show some wear and tear. And sometimes there's just nothing you can do about it.

However, a rustic building space does not mean you can let things fall apart on the inside. Despite the supplies lining the hallways for your fundraising event, despite the stacks of paper needed for your educational workshops, despite the myriad files you must keep to satisfy government regulations, keep it clean.

Your space reflects your culture and your level of professionalism. It sends an intuitive message to every single person who walks in your door about the way you go about your business. It insinuates how effective and efficient you are. It lets your customers know whether or not you take your organization seriously.

If you don't reflect that you take yourself seriously, why should they?

Refresh the painting of your walls every so often, and make sure the colors match. Try to replace crumbling office furniture. Don't be afraid to throw stuff away. Give staff a half day once each quarter to clean out their spaces and do a dump. Get the junk out of your hallways, and don't let dying plants stay in your lobby.

Grassroots doesn't equal dirty offices. And for donors who are investing in you, volunteers who are giving their time, and customers who want to be served by you, a dirty office can feel pretty crummy.

The Beauty of Customer Service...

is that we are all customers, all the time. Think of your best-ever customer service experience. Then remember a situation when you had a terrible experience and didn't return. Schedule a training and get your staff and volunteers to do the same exercise. Create a statement or value proposition around your customer service. Pinpoint ten new customer service steps you'll take with your organization starting tomorrow.

Your organization will be better for it.

Chapter 19

HOW TO BE A GREAT NONPROFIT LEADER

If you've read this book straight through to this chapter, we've worked through a lot of issues. We've talked about how to set up systems, how to create a more functional board experience, and how to manage your staff effectively. We've explored founder issues and volunteer issues and customer service issues.

We've covered a lot about how to manage your nonprofit.

Now it's time to talk about how to *lead* it.

Chances are you're already a good leader. That's why you're reading books like this one—because you want to run your organization better, grow it, make more of a difference, do good *well*.

That's the sign of a good leader right there.

Now we turn to the topic of *great* leaders—and how to become one.

When you really look around, it's a relatively small group. But that doesn't mean you can't be part of it. This next section has some clues on how to get there. I believe you're already on your way.

The Forest Versus the Trees

Great leaders know they have tremendous skill. They know where their strengths lie. They also know where there might be gaps, and they have the smarts to surround themselves with others who can fill them.

One way to grow as a leader is to figure out just what kind of leader you are—and how to supplement what you bring to the proverbial table.

You do this through introspection, reflection, and self-assessment. And you begin by taking a look at my Forest versus Trees Theory.

It goes like this: There are two kinds of people in this world—forest people and trees people. Forest people prefer to survey the lay of the land before they dive into anything. When they travel, they get the big map of the city, the state, and the country, and figure out the general way things fit together before venturing off. They read through instructions before starting on a project. They have to-do lists and review them often. They like to get a look at the strategic plan before entering a nonprofit organization. Then, once they have their context, they begin to visit the trees, to get a sense of the details, how the pieces fit together, discovering the nuances along the way.

Trees people enter into a situation by first encountering the pieces and then figuring out how they go together. Their comfort zone is getting to know the details, sometimes intimately, and then using that knowledge to rise up to that 40,000-foot view for a sense of the terrain. When they travel, they emerge from the train station and start down a random street, figuring out the twists and turns along the way. Trees people begin instruction manuals with step one and patiently follow each step, with the knowledge that they will complete the project to its perfect ending. They display Post-it notes around their computers, doing tasks one at a time and tackling them with concentrated fervor. They get to know a nonprofit organization by walking in the door and talking to people about their work. They thrive on every detail and ask a lot of questions.

Forest people learn about the departments within a nonprofit by looking at its organizational chart. Trees people meet staff members and find out which department they work in. Forest people love strategy and tend to be impatient with the day-to-day. Trees people excel at implementation and don't spend as much time thinking about the strategy tying all the pieces together.

Neither forest nor trees people are better than the other. And there is a wide spectrum. Some people are blatantly forest and some are decisively trees. Still others fall near the middle somewhere, and really honor both the system and the pieces within it. I will say, however, that nobody I've encountered is exactly 50/50—everyone skews to one side. This means you do, too.

Me? I am forest. I am, in actuality, painfully forest—and it can hurt me if I'm not careful. I do not like to start a project until I know the goal, the players, and the timeline, yet sometimes those aren't yet defined. I don't have a whole lot of patience for lengthy processes, so I've been known to rush through them. I don't love details, so I can skip them if I'm not careful. I might think people just know where I am coming from on a decision, so I don't explain it enough. It was only when I ran across trees people and, subsequently, made their collective heads spin—and also didn't find the ultimate success I wanted—that I recognized my incredibly heavy forest skewing.

Hubby? Total trees guy. My husband will happily wander through a new city, memorizing the streets and routes as he goes until he figures out the neighborhoods. He loves Post-it notes because he can surround himself with details and tackle each new surprise. He comes up with innovative and creative ideas that can be fostered only through processing, brainstorming, and a good dose of rumination. The problem is that sometimes they are not a good use of his time—or his energy.

I work on a prioritized hierarchy of lists and projects, where I stubbornly focus on the "important" stuff and may blow off the rest. His plate tends to be flatter, where everything has equal weight and it's hard to get things off it.

Neither of us is right. Neither of us is wrong. We are just different.

And both of us are necessary to get things done.

The important thing is knowing, first, where you fall, and then, where those around you do, too. If you recognize your category and work with others to supplement you, you can help each other. If you blow it off or think you're better, you can and will drive each other crazy. It's your choice.

If you are a forest person, you need to think about what details and processes you could be skipping without even knowing it. Find a few trees people and ask them to call you on the pieces you might be missing. If you are a trees person, chances are you'll get the details done every time, but you could lose sight of your goal or get mired in minutia that really don't matter. Find tricks or people to help keep your proverbial eyes on that proverbial prize—to remember what you're fighting for.

Forest and trees people can get on each other's nerves and drive each other a bit crazy. Try not to let this happen. I had a staff member who was a trees person through and through. In the beginning I was frustrated by her. Why was she always playing devil's advocate, pulling out the pitfalls of my master plans? Why was she always overwhelmed? Why was she such a perfectionist? Didn't she know we just needed to get stuff done?

Things were no better for her. Why didn't I ever explain my thinking? Why did I rush ahead with strategies without thinking things through? How could I push projects forward without finishing all of the pieces?

Once we figured out who we were, things got easier. Even though we could still grate on each other a bit, we could at least identify why that was, suspend judgment, and use each other to our mutual benefit. I would run my plans by her to figure out what I was missing. She would come to me when she got overwhelmed to sort through her projects and determine what really mattered.

Know who you are. Know what this means. Then find others to supplement or complement what you've got.

I challenge you now to reflect on this—on you.

THE FOREST PEOPLE

Your strengths are:
- You get results more quickly by staying focused and driving forward.
- You don't waste time on mundane details.
- You create and keep momentum by constantly moving things ahead.

Your cautionary tales:
- You skip details that might be important.
- You don't always think things through to assess all implications of your actions.
- You fail to involve people or portions of the process that are important and might lose buy-in.

THE TREES PEOPLE

Your strengths are:
- You don't miss details and may find better success when you get to your endgame.
- You involve the necessary people in the process to get buy-in.
- You have an intimate knowledge of the projects you work on.

Your cautionary tales:
- You are prone to "analysis paralysis"—getting stuck in the details, unsure how to move forward.
- Your results come more slowly.
- You might lose sight of the goals, or lose time by focusing on less important matters and getting burned out more quickly.

Again, neither is right or wrong. What's important is to know who you are, how to use your strengths, and how to mitigate your cautionary tales.

One Final Word: How to Talk to Each Other

Forest and Trees people don't just act differently; they also speak differently. In fact, sometimes it feels as though they speak different languages altogether.

- Do you speak in wide, sweeping terms? Or do you talk about the steps needed to get to where you're going?
- Do you say things like, "We'll figure it out when we get there," or do you find yourself saying things like, "Wait, let's take a step back before we push this forward"?
- Do you talk broadly about your goals, or do you focus on the day-to-day tasks that need to get done?
- Do you find yourself so excited about an idea that you can't understand why others won't get on board? Or do you find yourself frustrated by people who seem so irresponsible as to come up with an idea without knowing for sure that it's feasible?

Know that being a forest or trees person informs your action and your language. Know which one you are, and understand how you speak as a result. And know that, like it or not, you will need to adapt your words and your actions to those around you.

Chapter 20

COMMUNICATION

Communication is one of those broad terms that seems to be used all the time but really doesn't mean much to people. It's also something that most people assume they are good at, but few people have really mastered.

In theory, communication should be pretty easy. Most of us speak the same language as those around us, and most of us know what we want. Most of us like to talk to people. And even if we're not that crazy about it, we spend hours of our day communicating, verbally and nonverbally, through our spoken words and our written ones.

Yet every day we find that people we thought we were so in sync with actually have a completely different understanding of our goals, our work, and our plans.

- We set up a meeting with a potential donor who shows up with absolutely no clue that we're about to ask her for a major gift.
- We have a half-hour phone conversation with a board member about the budget, and then he acts surprised at the board meeting when the spreadsheet is sent around.
- We talk about the new dress code banning graphic T-shirts, and a staff member shows up wearing one the very next day.

It happens every day, in every kind of relationship.

Sometimes I'll ask my husband what feels to me like the most direct question in the world—about something benign, such as what we'll do with our Saturday or whether or not we plan to eat out that evening—and a few hours later he's pulling on a jacket and I'm in my PJs and we're both wondering what the other person is up to.

What happened? A few things.

Issue 1. We talk differently.

We all have different experiences, and different ways of expressing what we're thinking or feeling. As a result, we define words differently, even the obvious ones. I use the word *overwhelmed* only when I feel as if I'm about to have a nervous breakdown. On the other hand, I had a staff member who used it regularly to indicate she was busy. For years, no matter how hard I worked with her on time management, I could never figure out why she couldn't get herself more stabilized. Then I realized she actually was—we were just talking differently.

Issue 2. We hint.

Another factor in the communication gap is that we tend to use a lot of subtext, often without a clue that we're doing so.

Going back to *overwhelmed*, if I tell my husband that's how I'm feeling, chances are I want to talk about what's going on so he can help me work through it. I just expect him to know this, and then feel hurt or angry when he nods and makes a sympathetic face, then returns to eating his turkey burger and watching his favorite TV show.

We all use subtext when we communicate. We do it through our nonverbals and we do it through our word choices. We also do it when we choose not to communicate at all—when we don't return an email that offended us and figure the other person will just know that, well, he or she has offended us.

We often think this communication will be as clear as a bell to the receiver, but the truth is that it's often a blurry mess. Why? Because people don't speak our code or our special language. We haven't let them in on our irony or the way we intonate when we're joking versus when we're being perfectly serious. And so they don't get our hints.

Why would they?

Issue 3. We avoid conflict.

I say this again: *Nobody* really likes conflict, and this is especially true in the nonprofit world. We are kind, passionate people. We don't like to hurt people's feelings, nor put ourselves in a position where we might make somebody angry.

And so we do that dance, where we hint and hope that they get our meaning.

- We ask our board chair to get that direct mail letter signed "when he can," when we actually plan to send it out two days from now.
- We feel angry at our colleagues in a meeting, and so we clam up and expect them to change their behavior.
- We want to ask prospective donors for $5,000 but we're uncomfortable with the amount, so we show them the Give Now! form and let them complete it, which they do— for $500.

Issue 4. We don't pay attention.

Some of us have gotten very good (or think we have, anyway) at pretending to listen to others when, in reality, we're actually thinking about that meeting with our boss at the end of the day or booking a mental ticket for our upcoming vacation.

We do it with emails, too. We get a message that provides all kinds of important updates about a project, and we scan it, skim it, and move on.

We are in a culture in which it's easier than ever to be distracted, where focus is actually, almost physically, difficult for us. But if we don't pay attention, if we aren't present in the moment, we will lose the details of what is being said, what is being asked of us. We get frustrated when others fail to come through after we feel we've been so clear. But this is a two-way street, and we're guilty of the same thing.

The sooner we realize we can't half-focus and get away with it, the sooner we realize it makes us less effective, and the sooner we decide this is unacceptable, the sooner we do better for our organizations.

Miscommunication happens regularly—every day, perhaps every hour—for the reasons listed here along with myriad others. So what can you do about it?

The Key to Communication

There are many solutions, but I'm going to focus on the one tip that works in every situation. It clarifies expectations, wants, and needs, and decreases the confusion caused by the various perspectives, definitions, and styles at the table.

I can sum it up in two words: Be explicit.

Explicit language is contextual language. It doesn't include subtext and it doesn't hint. It doesn't hope that the other person will get what we're trying to say. Instead, it ensures it because, well, we're *saying* it.

Let me give you an example.

When hubby and I first moved to San Diego, I was in a vulnerable place.

We'd moved because he'd been promoted. He was moving up in the world. Me? I was jobless. Having just come off my position as executive director of a large nonprofit, I had to face facts: I was now pretty unimportant. I was also, all of a sudden, definitively, desperately needy.

The mornings were okay. I kept myself busy networking and exploring our new city. But by mid-afternoon, it was all over. I was antsy. I was anxious. I was cranky. I realized I needed an emotional hand from hubby. And so I told him so.

At least I thought I did. I told him the afternoons were torture for me, that I needed to talk with someone, that I would love to hear from him if he got the chance.

The next day he didn't call. At first I was angry, hurt that he didn't care.

But then I realized what I'd done wrong. So that evening I said the following to him:

"You know, by about 2:30 in the afternoon I've reached my emotional limit and I feel very lonely. So I need you to call me at that time and just check in for a few minutes."

The next day he called. Right at 2:30.

Why did he do it? Not because he all of a sudden got me in a whole new way. Not because he'd grown smarter or I'd grown telepathic in the last 24 hours. Not because he cared about me more than he had the day before.

He did it because I'd been explicit. Being explicit means stating—clearly—what you need, what you want, and what you expect. It means leaving nothing implied. Nothing to chance.

It means you have increased your odds of getting what you want—from your staff, from your boss, from your partner, from your friends.

Being explicit does *not* mean being tactless. You can be explicit while still showing a level of engagement that fits the person with whom you're speaking. You can be appropriate. You can be smart about it. You can be compassionate. You can be interesting. Just be clear, too.

There are far too many important things going on at your nonprofit to leave things to interpretation. Learn to be explicit, and to do it well, and if nothing else, everyone will know exactly what you need, want, or expect.

In many cases, they'll even deliver.

Chapter 21

TIME MANAGEMENT

You could have the greatest, most intentional goals, the money to make them happen, and the inspired staff and board to get them there, and yet a seemingly small detail can cause it all to go to pieces, falling away like your greatest dreams, causing all kinds of frustrations and turning your perfect strategies into chaos.

It's what happens when you don't manage your time well.

You know the drill: You walk into work in the morning with all kinds of plans about what you will get done, deadlines you need to meet, new ideas you want to research, inspiring messages you plan to write. You just know today will be the day you finally develop that template for board orientation or call those donors who haven't yet sent in this year's gift.

And…within 45 minutes your good intentions have become a distant memory.

Why? Because you've become embroiled in all kinds of issues that popped up, seemingly overnight. And they all need to be addressed now. Your board member called about an agenda item for the upcoming meeting. Your development director needs changes to the year-end appeal so it can be sent out. Your program manager needs to discipline her staff and calls you for guidance.

This kind of thing happens *all the time*, and to just about everyone in both the for-profit and the nonprofit sectors. It's human nature to lose focus and time—to be reactive, to address a newly emerged crisis, to get stuck in some kind of chitchat pit with staff. It's also human nature to focus on what makes you comfortable—answering one more email, taking a walk to the break room to connect with staff. Let's be honest—these things are a whole lot easier than figuring out your new outcome measurement strategy.

And while all of this is common and makes us human, it also makes you less effective as a leader. Projects get pushed, deadlines get missed, and money doesn't come in. If nothing else, you aren't moving forward with new initiatives or plans, and you're relying on what you know to get you through the day. Plus—and I've seen this with almost every person I've coached—issues with time management lead to all kinds of stress. The work piles up but you can't get any of it off your plate, and you wind up driving home at the end of the day feeling as if you got nothing done, and berating yourself for failing to reach your goals.

Tackle the Time Management Monster

The good news is that there are things—some of them fairly simple—that you can do to improve your time management dysfunction. Immediately.

Here are just a few:

Tip 1. Find an organizational system that works for you and commit to it. As with so many other things, you need to set yourself up for success. In matters of time management, this means finding an organizational system that works for your style. Some people love electronic calendars and task lists. Some believe in the tactile nature of a paper file system or organizer. Others love their hand-held devices. Some use notebooks. Others love legal pads.

None of these are right are wrong, but they will be right or wrong *for you*. You know yourself best, and so you need to think through what is and isn't working about your current organization system and adapt it accordingly. And if your new system doesn't work, you need to move on to something else.

I learned this the hard way—by first choosing a system that was all wrong for me. I got my hands on a cool little electronic device, expecting it to be the answer to my time management prayers. Instead, I found that punching in all of those keys and trying to make sense of those funny-looking dots on my digital screen caused all kinds of additional stress. So I returned to paper.

Everyone is different. This isn't about creating a system that works for your colleague or using a new piece of technology that your board member swears by. It's about what will work for you. You are in charge of setting yourself up for your own success, and you know yourself best. So do it.

Tip 2. Close your door.

If you find you are easily distracted and need to concentrate on a project, close your door. Yes, connecting with staff is important. But know when it is, versus when it's just your way of putting something off. Be intentional both when you close your door and when you leave it open. And don't be afraid to tell people why you're doing either.

This tip, of course, assumes that you actually have an office door. I've also worked in companies where it was all cubicles, all the time. In that case you need to find another way. Go to a coffee shop and work from there, or work from home for a few hours. Again, figure out what works for you. Then do it.

Tip 3. What's a crisis, really?

The nonprofit sector in particular is great at the crisis mentality.

Everything feels like an emergency. Funders need statistics today, and boards need their questions answered today. Clients are calling you and your staff is feeling overwhelmed. Today.

What many people don't realize is that just because someone makes a last-minute request or claims to have an urgent matter to be addressed doesn't make it an emergency. Before you buy into someone else's high-pitched crisis mentality, and before you find yourself making that crisis yours, take a second to ask yourself if this is *really* a crisis, and if you really need to be involved. Ask yourself if you really need to drop your plans for the day to handle it immediately.

And know when you, yourself, are calling something a crisis when it's not. Ask yourself if you're doing it because it truly does feel serious, because you need to focus on something else, or because dealing with a crisis makes you feel like you're being a good leader.

Nonprofits tend to get dramatic around the idea of crises. When staff members come to you with a so-called crisis, ask yourself if this is really an emergency or if you might call it something else. Is it instead a hard-pressed deadline? An important issue to be addressed? A serious decision that needs to be made? Then treat it that way.

Engage in this redefining exercise and you'll learn pretty quickly how much of what you used to think was a crisis is actually just one more day-to-day nonprofit occurrence. It might still need to be addressed, but chances are you have a bit more flexibility fitting it into your schedule than you previously would have thought.

Tip 4. Keep the chatter to a minimum.
One of the reasons we work in nonprofits is because the people are incredible. They are passionate, they are dedicated, and they love to connect with other people.

It's what makes us effective. It's also what makes us inefficient.

Once I left the office environment and struck out on my own, I was surprised by how many different projects I could tackle in a day. I realized this was because I was alone. I couldn't distract myself by wandering down the hall, where I might pass a half dozen people with whom I could have an unscheduled conversation.

These days my work begins precisely at the start of the day, not 45 minutes after I arrive at the office, after catching up on somebody's weekend. My lunches are strategic, not an opportunity to make new friends. My day ends when the work is done, not when the clock shows we've got about 20 minutes left so starting a new project doesn't make a whole lot of sense.

When we work in a traditional office, when we wonder why we can't seem to get things done, we must think about how much of our time we spend on the casual conversations. On the friendships. On the chatter.

There's nothing wrong with this...to a point. Your colleagues are great. And everybody does it.

But...

I challenge you to do the following. Take one week and assess how much time you spend talking to others about things that have nothing to do with your projects.

If you find you're losing hours, observe your patterns and force yourself to change them. Don't put your food in the kitchen fridge at the start of the day if everyone is congregated there and you wind up talking for a half hour. Don't walk down the hallway where you know temptation lies in the form of your favorite, chatty co-workers.

Tip 5. Remember.

We all know that feeling that burns in our stomachs when it's clear we have missed or are about to miss a deadline. We know how much we hate it when we have to work late into the night because a board report is due the next day. We know it in the moment, but we forget it.

Don't.

How does it feel when you can't be home with family or out with friends because you're finishing up a project? How does it feel to do something last minute, when you know you could have done it better if you'd just given it more time?

Describe it in detail to yourself. Right now. Then remember it. Draw a picture or write it down if you need to. Then reflect on it when you are tempted to allow distractions to get in the way.

Tip 6. Tell others you're working on this.

If you decide this is an issue and you know you will have a hard time resisting distractions, ask your co-workers to keep you honest. Know who will support you and who has the incentive to sabotage you because they're not good at time management either. Plan ahead with your meetings and your day. Write out your schedule— by the hour if necessary. Take responsibility for your actions. Trust the situation will get better. You will succeed.

THE TIME-SUCKING LIE WE TELL OURSELVES

When I'm working with nonprofit executives, the issue of time management always, *always* comes up. Their frustration in not having enough hours in the workday, in not getting things done, eats away at them. And so we go about assessing just how that workday is spent. That's when our greatest foe pops up. It's inevitable, it's a time-suck, and it's very, very real.

Email.

Now, I completely get that email is important. But let's get real about it. I was recently sitting among a group of professionals and someone asked how we'd all feel if we opened up our email and there was nothing new there.

We all chuckled, dramatically clasped our hands toward the sky, and said, *"If that could only be true!"*

• How much more time we could have!

• How much more focus we could have!

• How much more work we could get done!

Then, this person asked us again. And he asked us to be honest. I will go first.

If I were to open up my email in-box tomorrow and it came up empty, my heart would sink. Email is my way of connecting with my colleagues, with my clients, and with the circle of people I have worked so hard to find throughout my lifetime.

An empty in-box might mean nobody cared enough to write me. Perhaps I'm not that important. And even though I'd know deep down that wasn't *really* the case, the emptiness of my in-box would be hard to swallow.

So now I ask you to think about the question, then recognize that our constant and deliberate decision to check our email in-boxes at every turn, thinking we're being so sly that nobody will notice we're doing it (when everyone does, by the way), is not necessarily about trying to stay on top of everything, though that's a fantastic excuse.

In reality, for many of us, email is our way of connecting, of communicating, of being validated. It's also our way of focusing on something else when the job gets too tough, the project too tedious, the stress level too high. It's the perfect, most devious distraction. And it's common.

But once we are honest with ourselves we can admit that there are very, very few things in that in-box that need our immediate attention. If someone must reach you *now* about a pressing issue, that person will follow up with a phone call *now*.

And when we think about how many hours we spend in a day focusing on emails instead of our projects, letting our minds wander to what's new instead of what's in front of us—or what we don't want to deal with—then at least we can work toward having some discipline in the matter.

I challenge you to acknowledge the big email lie, and resist the urge to check it incessantly. Keep your email program closed until you are ready to check it. Then designate a time to do so.

Start out by checking it every hour, maybe every half hour until you get used to it. Use that other time—the time previously sucked up—to get your work done, progress toward your strategies, and get home at a decent hour.

Do it for a week.

Then sit back and revel in all of that you've achieved.

Chapter 22

THE SINGLE BEST THING YOU CAN DO TO IMPROVE YOUR WORK LIFE

I've realized over time that there is an emotion that I hate more than any other—more than anger or sadness or fear.

Disappointment.

I call it the "D word." I hate feeling let down. And I hate it even more when people feel the "D word" about me.

Sometimes we can't avoid disappointment. Sometimes there is something we are so sure is going to happen—we're going to get a grant, or a new hire is going to be the perfect fit, or our golf tournament will absolutely make budget this time—*we just know it!* And then it doesn't happen and we're sure we can feel our hearts sink a bit into our bellies.

But one thing I've learned is that there are many, many other times when we set ourselves up for disappointment. And we do it over and over again, often in the same ways, over the same issues.

Why does this happen? And how do we avoid it?

Here is what I propose.

The single best thing you can do to improve your life at your nonprofit is to change your expectations.

I stop here because I just know what many of you are thinking. *I cannot expect less than the absolute best for my nonprofit! We will never be great if I do that!*

So let me be clear. I am *not* saying to lower your expectations for your nonprofit and its goals, mission, and systems. I am *not* saying you should settle for the status quo or, even worse, that you shouldn't aim for excellence, growth, or new achievements.

Accept the Truths You Already Know

What I am saying is that there are some absolute truths in working in the nonprofit sector, and for some reason we have a very hard time accepting them.

And so we continue to set ourselves up for disappointment, heartache, and frustration. Because we believe they will change. And they won't. The sooner you know these truths, accept them, and figure out how to work around them, the sooner your disappointment and frustration levels will go down. It's that simple.

I present these truths to you now.

Universal Truth 1: Your board is not going to embrace fundraising.
Recently I was providing a training about boards to a group of nonprofit professionals. One of them raised his hand and asked me the following: "How do I get my board to like and embrace fundraising?"

The entire group leaned forward, expectantly. They were all looking for the perfect answer, the magic bullet. But it didn't come.

Because my answer was, very simply, "They won't."

Why won't they? And what's up with board members not wanting to get their contacts to give money? And how can you define the board's fundraising role in a way that sets the organization up for success, the board up for doing their job, and you up for far less frustration? It's all covered in the money section. (See page 193.)

For now, just know this universal truth, even though you might not agree with it. Change your expectation, manage this process as best you can, and let yourself feel a little less heated when those board fundraising initiatives don't come through.

Universal Truth 2: Your staff is going to take things personally.
You can make the most logical, strategic decisions in the world, and relate them carefully to the staff, explaining the reasons behind your choices and why they aren't personal.

It won't matter.

You can discuss someone's performance in the most quantitative and professional terms possible.

It won't matter.

You can try to include every single person in a big speech where you thank them for their hard work at an event, taking special care to mention everyone by first name.

It won't matter.

You can talk about reducing the amount of bananas in the food bank because the cost of produce has gone way up.

It won't matter.

By nature we take things personally. At nonprofits we do it even more so.

Why?

Remember the Mission Myth. Remember that nonprofits, by nature, attract passion. They attract emotion. They attract tireless commitment. And all of those proverbial hearts on proverbial sleeves tend to take things personally.

So change your expectations.

Knowing up front that this is part of the nonprofit makeup will not make it go away. It will, however, keep you from feeling quite so frustrated when you've done everything in your power to be clear and respectful and you still need to call a team meeting to work through the tears.

It will help you manage the situation by planning ahead on how you will respond.

And it will allow you to feel justified in your decisions, even when it feels terrible because everyone around you is up in arms.

Universal Truth 3: You cannot convince everybody to care about or give to your organization.

This is a trap for many of us. We sincerely believe that if we just talk about our organization enough, people will *get it*, and they will want to give to it, volunteer for it, and commit themselves to it.

It's just not the reality.

Think about a group of your friends. Each of them has different interests, different experiences, and different priorities in life. You can talk about your cause all evening, but that doesn't mean you'll convert them. Because they will then talk about what matters to them. And we each have the right to care about our own passions and focus on our own priorities.

We in the nonprofit sector care deeply about our organizations. Chances are, because we work for them, serve on their boards, or volunteer for them, we care more than just about anybody else. And so we think we can get everyone else to do the same.

If we talk about our cause and why it matters, will people take notice and feel something in the moment? Probably.

Will they commit themselves to the organization in some way? Probably not.

We can be (and often are) incredibly inspiring when we talk about our organizations. And in the end, we just need to understand that others won't care about it as much as we do.

That's why we're there. And they're not.

Universal Truth 4: Finances are part of your life—and they aren't always pretty.

If you take a job in a nonprofit in any kind of management role, money will be a permanent part of your life. You will not be able to shake this truth, so don't try.

But many managers do. They are somehow under the misconception that since their cash flow is okay *now,* they have a great development director *now,* and their accounting is in line *now,* they can forget about the money issue for a while.

First of all, if you've accomplished everything in that previous paragraph, hats off to you. You are in a teeny, tiny minority. Yet even then it is still up to you to know your budget inside and out, how it's tracking, and what the plans are for current stability and future growth.

For the rest of us where things aren't quite so grand, it's even clearer that money must always be one of our main focus areas. Yet many of us—especially the majority who have not made financial learning part of our life—hope we can just get the right people in the right seats, watch our fundraising plans go full speed, and worry about the financial situation once a month when the treasurer delivers the finance report at the board meeting.

Here's the truth: Money is dynamic. Funders change their focus areas or lose money themselves. Major donors move on to other causes and other regions. Development staff and financial staff get new jobs. Prices go up.

So even if things are good right this minute, you must as a leader do your best to ensure things stay this way. You must be part of the budgeting process, you must understand how to read an income statement, you must have a sense of how much is in each of your bank accounts, you must think strategically about your fundraising strategies and their future potential.

And you must change your expectations. Because once you embrace the messy truth that money will not always come in as expected, that funding will go away, that events will be a bust, and that new projects aren't that enticing to your favorite grantors—once you know this, you will be prepared to handle it. Which is what you need to do.

Universal Truth 5: You will screw up.
I hated this one when I first came to it. And I came to it hard.

I'd never shown signs of perfectionism before taking on my role as ED. I always knew I had faults and things to learn, and I always knew I'd make mistakes.

Yet when I made them at my nonprofit, the mistakes felt heavier. After all, when I screwed up in this role I was hurting people with AIDS.

144

And make no mistake, I screwed up a lot (which is obvious, since that's what this whole book is about!). And frankly, I needed to. It's how I learned my greatest lessons, and I became a stronger leader as a result.

I screwed up in all kinds of ways:

- I screwed up by not engaging my board enough.
- I screwed up by making bad hires.
- I screwed up by not learning how to read a balance sheet more quickly.
- I screwed up by cutting budgets too much, and then too little.
- I screwed up vacation accrual policies.
- I screwed up staff retreat agendas.

And here's the other truth: None of those screw-ups hurt people with AIDS. Did they hurt my pride? Sure. Did they hurt the staff or our efficiencies or our day-to-day operations? Sometimes. But we always recovered.

Everyone makes mistakes. You need to know you will. Learn the things you don't know, plan ahead, and do the best job you can every day. And when those inevitable screw-ups happen, recognize them, own them, fix them, and move on.

The other important thing you can do? Expect them.

Have you ever met a person in your life who has never, ever erred? No. So don't put yourself in an unreasonable and unfeasible position and think that you'll be the first.

Universal Truth 6: The board dynamic is messy.
I come back around to the board because it is such an ever-present, challenging dynamic for each and every nonprofit I've ever encountered.

We've already spent plenty of time exploring the reasons behind this issue and how to manage it (see pages 48), so I won't dive into all of the details again. What I will say is that I've seen far, far too many EDs come away from a few good board meetings—or who at the time truly have an incredibly functional board—and let their guard down, thinking that this board thing is *fixed*. It is *fine*.

It's not possible.

Even the most functional boards will need to address financial issues. They will need to update mission statements. They will need to review the ED. They will need to have difficult conversations and make hard, often unpopular decisions. And members will be stepping off—and on—the board at regular intervals.

By nature, the board relationship—with the staff and itself—is messy. So change your expectations that the board relationship can ever be perfect or fixed. It's as dynamic as running water, ebbing and flowing as the organization evolves.

And know that you need to be a part of managing the board, setting it up for success and strategizing its future. It's part of your job, whether you like it or not.

Chapter 23

THE IMPORTANCE OF REDEFINING SUCCESS

While a good portion of this book—including the last section—is about the many, nuanced challenges of running a nonprofit, I also want to assure you that you will have successes.

- You'll score a big donation and exceed the expected goal of a new program.
- You'll get a grant from a new funder and you'll find a fantastic new board member.
- You'll get a front-page story in the paper and your event will go off without a hitch.

Even though much of your role as a leader is to give away credit and take the blame, please, please, please celebrate these successes. Pat yourself on the back, tell your spouse or friends about it, and let them tell you that you did a great job.

You need to acknowledge the things that go well, because you will definitely hear about the things that don't.

Which can feel somewhat defeating. You might not get tons of kudos for the good things because they are somewhat expected. The bad things, however, every single little detail it seems, will be related to you.

The trick, of course, is to ensure that you keep some perspective on all of this, that you don't allow yourself to feel too lousy about yourself, the job, or both.

How to do this?

Redefine What Success Means

Many successes, like the ones I listed above, will be obvious. Many, however, will not.

Too often good leaders fixate on those big wins, the external validation that comes with an endgame like a funding check or a programmatic outcome. They don't recognize all of the things they did along the way—things that were hard, things that others wouldn't have done or thought to do—that also make a difference for the organization. And they certainly don't recognize the things that, at first blush, feel awfully negative, such as a disciplinary conversation with a staff member or turning down funding for a project that isn't the right fit. In reality, these moments of high "ick," where one is tested and must make hard decisions for the good of the cause, are not only some of your greatest successes. They also reflect some of your grandest moments of leadership.

Success means all kinds of things:
- It means taking something risky on and letting something painful go.
- It means having a hard conversation with a staff member and doing it well.
- It means waking up early to go to the gym when you haven't before.

I always ask my coaching clients to log their successes each day, and I stress that we are not just talking about the obvious ones. It forces them to take note, if just for a minute, of what they've done to move themselves or their organizations forward. Over time they start to redefine success for themselves. They begin to acknowledge their work. They sit up straighter. They are more confident. And, in the end, they become better leaders.

What did you do today to move a strategy forward? What have you been meaning to tackle that you finally got off your list? What did you say to someone that represented your organization well? How did you take care of yourself in a new way?

Should you go out and boast about all of these things? No. And you won't, because you're a strong leader and you know that you don't ever want to appear arrogant. But you should acknowledge them to yourself, and maybe to your SWAT Team. (See page 151.)

If nothing else, take one second to tell yourself that you just did something well. Then take a breath, and move on to the next thing.

Chapter 24

A SPECIAL NOTE FOR THE ED: HOW TO SURVIVE THE LONELIEST JOB

I've been one. I've reported to one. I've overseen one. And so I can honestly say this about the executive director position:

It's tough.

I mean *am-I-crazy-for-doing-this?* tough. And, when done correctly, it's also very, very lonely.

I equate the ED job to the center of an hourglass. You, as the ED, are right there in the middle, trying to meet a mission effectively, overseen by the top of the hourglass, your board. At the bottom are your other stakeholders, and there are many: staff, volunteers, clients, funders.

Everyone has an expectation. Everyone needs you now. Everyone merits attention. And to do the job well, you need to be on top of it all every day—keeping your eye on the strategy but not letting any details fall through the proverbial cracks. Being responsive to every message and fully present for every meeting, completely grasping all of the various programmatic, fundraising, and financial components of the organization. Giving away the credit and taking the blame.

And through it all, having the finesse, the savvy, and the grace to make it seem like it's all under control, that you like and respect every single person you come across, and that your passion and commitment are unwavering.

That's the reason it's hard.

The reason it's lonely is that you can't really tell anyone how hard it is.

You put yourself in a terrible position if you complain to your board or bring them problems without solutions. And you put your organization in a terrible position if you complain to anyone else. Your staff isn't paid enough to take on your cash flow issues, and talking too much about your board woes with internal or external individuals will only shake their confidence in you and your organization.

So there you are.

Don't get me wrong, being the top executive comes with its benefits: more power, prestige, and pay than most everyone else in your organization. It's just that nobody else gets the rest of it—the tough stuff—and no one really can who hasn't been there.

ED Survival 101

So how do you keep yourself both effective and sane throughout this rewarding, challenging, lonely ordeal?

Survival Tip 1: Create your SWAT Team.
You need a team of people on the outside who are there for you. This can be a challenging task if your work life is pretty much your whole life, yet it's vital. It also takes strategy. Don't begin talking to the guy next to you at the gym and think he's going to give you what you need. Don't choose friends known to be overly critical, competitive, and judgmental. And don't just create a team of advocates who all think you can do no wrong and will automatically blame the other guy for your woes.

You need a mix of people who are on your side, who you can trust with your vulnerability, and who will give it to you straight. You need to think your SWAT Team through—not just when you're putting it together in your head but as you get ready to reach out to one of its members for a specific purpose.

My SWAT Team is made up of the following:
- When I need an advocate to whine to and who will always be on my side: my mother

- When I need someone who respects me, gives me the benefit of the doubt, and will objectively tell me the truth about a situation: my husband
- When I need someone who will take a very critical eye toward my actions and sometimes be a bit harsh: my friend Joe
- When I need someone who will give me an opinion but will do so very kindly and gently because I'm particularly vulnerable: my coach
- When I need people to look out for my physical, emotional, and mental well-being: my weight-training partners.
- When I need legal advice: my lawyer
- When I need financial advice: my accountant

There are certainly others I speak with in a time of need, but this SWAT Team is my touchstone. These are people who have no need to lie to me or to hold back on their opinions and advice, and they respect me and want me to be as successful as possible.

One of the most important things to remember as you create your SWAT Team is to consider who should *not* be on it. This isn't always obvious. Beware of those who seem like your friends but are competitors. And also be careful of one-uppers, as well as those who will tell you what you want to hear but don't necessarily believe it. Your SWAT Team is your sacred circle. Its members need to be on your side.

As an ED, think about your needs, and determine who meets them best. And then stick to your SWAT Team when you can— even telling them that they are members. Trust me—pick the right individuals and they will be flattered. And you'll find a whole new level of support you didn't know you had.

Survival Tip 2: Find other EDs you can trust.
Another method I found helpful was to reach out to others in the same position and just talk shop. We'd talk about our boards and

our staff, and ask each other for advice. Some were even part of competing organizations, but I trusted them. Trust is everything.

As we'd talk about our issues and shake our heads in amazement at the absurdity of some of the things we were dealing with, we couldn't help but smile a bit. Just knowing there are others who are going through something similar creates unmatched validation. We had "ED Survival Lunches" every other month. I can't tell you how much I looked forward to them.

Survival Tip 3: Get a coach.

Coaches and mentors have the benefit of being objective and, you hope, skilled at helping you discover your needs and the solutions to your problems. They can also help you figure out your own personal and professional goals in addition to the ones at your organization. Because coaches are there for *you*—as opposed to consultants hired to help your organization—your coach will be your advocate and confidante. That they're paid should also mean they are reliable and will follow up, and that they will provide resources and ask questions without judgment. I am a coach and I have a coach, and both are extremely fulfilling experiences.

Having a coach doesn't mean you're weak or bad at your job. It means you want to grow, get better, and stay sane. In fact, my first job as an executive coach is often to tell the executive that he or she is not crazy. My second is to let the client know that everything he or she is going through is perfectly normal and also quite common. It's amazing how just these first few points can create a whole new perspective for an ED. Just think about what might come after that.

Survival Tip 4: Get away.

Understand this: Your organization is not the sun. The world does not revolve around it. Its rewards and challenges are not the most important thing to every person. Yet when the messages and the tasks pile up and it seems as though you're drowning, when your organization isn't making budget and you're faced with laying people off, when your board calls or your event committee gets a new idea it wants to implement immediately, it's hard to remember this.

How *can* you remember this, and even believe it? Get away. Get on the outside looking in instead of the inside looking out, feeling like the whole world needs something from you right away. It doesn't. Yes, plenty of people do need you, but when you talk to others and see how other cities, states, and countries function, when you spend quality time breathing in the air, eating exotic foods, listening to different languages, you can't help but get perspective.

How do you keep this perspective when you get back? See Survival Tips 1 through 3.

One Final, Personal Note for EDs Everywhere

There's one more tip that I always give to every ED I work with. And now I give it to you.

First let me say that as an ED you are a special, special breed, working through a unique set of challenges that nobody else can really understand.

If you are reading this book, if you are seeking to better yourself and your organization, if you are a nonprofit executive dealing with the challenging, lonely culture that is organizational management, I ask you to take very seriously this next piece of advice:

Give yourself a break.

I say this with all sincerity. I say this in all seriousness.

I say this because you care about your organization, because you're introspective, because you are in it for the right reasons, because you are going to get better with each passing day.

You will not always be liked (see page 72), you will make mistakes (see page 144), and you will have wins (see page 147).

The best thing you can do every day…is your best. Make plans, think strategically, focus, stay organized, and learn.

And even though, through all of it, through each hard discussion with staff and each board meeting and each financial discussion, you might feel a bit of fear, don't let it hold you back.

Because here's the other thing to know:

Everyone is afraid.

Everybody. We are all afraid of the unknown. We are all afraid of failure. We are all afraid of messing up, of looking stupid, of failing. Some of us are just better at hiding it.

I know this because I've been around many, many powerful people in my lifetime. I've come across wealthy business people and elected officials. I've gotten to know powerful philanthropists and CEOs of multi-multimillion-dollar organizations.

I promise you, each and every one of them is afraid of something. I know because some told me. Others didn't, but their actions did.

For just a second, their insecurity came out. Perhaps it happened while they were busy telling me all they had accomplished. Perhaps it was while they were putting someone else down. Perhaps it was because they couldn't own any mistakes they'd made in the past.

Everyone is afraid.

So if you are, or if you're frustrated, or if your staff is talking about you behind closed doors and you're feeling as if you're the only one going through it all, know that it's common.

Know that you're doing the best job you can.

Know that you're making a difference for a very important cause.

And give yourself a break.

You've already been doing amazing things for a great cause. And, each day, you're just doing it better.

PART THREE

MONEY

Chapter 25

WHAT MONEY REALLY IS

Our first lessons about money shape our opinions about it for the rest of our lives.

Whether we come to know money as the definitive source of happiness, as a cause of family stress and shame, or as something we should always aim to have more of, we tend to believe it in our core, throughout our evolution, and into adulthood.

What Most People Think

Many nonprofits think of money as an evil, something that's not of true value. We are, after all, a *non*profit, working toward a mission, working for a higher purpose that means more than making a buck.

In our minds, money:

- Isn't a high priority.
- Represents all that is wrong with the rest of society.
- Is deserved by us, but nobody seems to know it.
- Is an issue we must tiptoe around with funders and donors.

The Truth

Money makes the mission, and so it is not just important, but a precious resource that must be honored and respected. Without money there is no strategy, there are no results, there is no real impact.

The truth is, money:

- Is a wonderful thing.
- Must be aggressively pursued.

- Is nothing to be ashamed of.
- Must be earned.

The Good News

It is possible to raise and manage money well.

You are seeking money on behalf of those you serve, and you have every right—no, you have an obligation—to go after it with all of your might, and spend it with honor and respect once you get it.

There are strategies to do this, but not everyone knows them. And some people know them but aren't very good at executing them. Which is why, when you figure them out, you're ahead of the game.

And so are the people you serve.

Chapter 26

PROVING YOUR WORTH TO FUNDERS

I've spent a lot of time talking to nonprofits about the four *Ms*, and no matter what, this is the one that always—*always*—comes up. It's not only one of the biggest needs of every organization, but also a top, very aggressive cause of anxiety for most, if not all, nonprofit managers.

When fundraising strategies don't meet budget and organizations seem to be hurtling toward their end-of-year without a plan to get back in the black, it's easy and understandable to have panic set in.

I've been there.

I've received those income statements, fresh off the printer, and looked immediately to that bottom right-hand corner to see if we were ahead or behind budget—then felt my heart sink as I got my answer. I've found, much to my dismay, that it's only the first quarter and I'm already way behind. I've felt that "ick" feeling in my gut as I tried to figure out just what else we might cut or what other development tactics we might add without seriously impacting the integrity of our work or frying out the fundraising staff.

Working through money issues takes strategy, careful planning, adaptation as you go, and a strong, skilled set of people to get those dollars in the door.

Many nonprofits believe fundraising is simply about letting others know about the important work they're doing and letting the money flow in.

We've all heard the cries from nonprofits.

There's a perfect storm, they say. There's increasing need and decreasing funding, and we need to keep our proverbial heads above the proverbial water. Help!

These nonprofits focus solely on getting philanthropists to understand why they need to give to their organizations. Why they *should* give.

To these nonprofits, I say…

Stop.

Don't *should* on anybody, especially a funder or a donor.

Because the truth is that nobody owes you anything.

It's hard for some people to swallow, but it's absolutely true. Yes, your mission is important, sometimes a matter of life and death for a certain group of people. It's clearly vitally important to the staff and board members who put their all into the organization on a regular basis.

But remember—nobody will love your organization as much, or be as passionate about it, as those of you working at it and for it. (See page 142.)

For those on the outside, there are many other important organizations also beating down their doors explaining why *they* are the most important cause in town, and why *they* are in that special situation that calls for the big gift *now*. The competition is fierce. And worthy.

Add to this the fact that the donors themselves have kids going to college and new credit card fees and car problems. They have many, many options for where to spend their money. They don't owe you anything. You must give them the reason not just to give to you, but to give to you *instead* of all of those other causes and situations fighting for their dollars.

We often think that if we can just get them to understand our plight, our work, our impact, *surely* they will give. I am here to tell you that getting gifts, getting larger gifts, and getting repeat gifts takes more than explaining the important work you do. Because as important as it is, there are others out there that are also important and that are targeting the same donors, creating the same fundraisers to gather them together, and employing the same tactics to get the money out of them.

The duty to make a strong argument as to why gifts should come to your organization instead of others doesn't stop with individual donors. The same goes for private foundations, community foundations, and the government. Yes, they are around to ensure people are being served. But they also have an obligation to make sure their money is going toward efforts that have the greatest impact, to organizations that do good *well*.

It's their job to make sure their dollars are being used in ways that are efficient, effective, and legal. It's their job to make sure that the money given on behalf of their stakeholders is being spent through policies that honor stewardship, transparency, and integrity.

This means it is up to you to prove you are doing all of these things every time. Nobody owes you. You have to convince every one of these entities that you are worthy of their money.

So how do you convince donors, foundations, and the government that your mission is critical *and* their dollars are being used with the highest levels of excellence?

First, by running like a business. By having clear goals and achieving impact. By having tracking and accounting systems in place that illustrate you spent their money in the way you promised. By setting up measurements that show the impact of their dollars. (See page 246.) By running legally, efficiently, and effectively.

Nobody owes you anything. But when you prove to funders that they should give their money to you because you spend it carefully and with integrity, with an eye toward specific goals, and with the *most results*, you up your odds of getting a gift not just now, but also in the future.

Chapter 27

THE FUNDRAISING PLAN

So you've proven to the funders that your mission is important, that you do good work toward predetermined goals, and that you will spend their money as promised. You've gotten yourself a check. Congratulations!

Now what does that mean, exactly? Have you reached your fundraising goal? Are you exceeding it? Should you raise your goal in a particular area? Are events your thing? Should you go after grants?

How will you know the answer to these questions?

Because you've created a plan that you will measure these things against, that will tell you everything you need to know.

When your organization puts together your strategic plan and clearly identifies your goals and objectives, you must then make sure the organization has a fundraising plan that clearly maps out how you will pay to reach them.

The plan is not simply the budget. It begins there, because the budget will tell you how much you need to raise for the year, then breaks it down by month. It will list each strategy (individual giving, private grants, membership dues, etc.) and how much money you believe you will raise in each.

The plan takes it from there.

- It begins with each strategy and breaks it down into extensive detail, including the tasks, deadlines, and point people for each project area.
- It creates understanding as to how each department, staff, and board member plays into the fundraising strategy.
- It defines how you will thank donors and input their information into your database.

- And, very importantly, it lays out how often the plan will be revisited, used to monitor the fundraising initiatives, and adjusted over time.

Use your favorite spreadsheet program to map it all out. Create a calendar so you know who is supposed to be doing what and when.

To raise money without a plan is to fly blind. It is to leave up to the universe, the stars, and the spirit of good luck that the money needed to fund the mission will simply come in.

This is not good enough. The money is the means to the very important end. But it *is* the means. To leave this lifeline to your mission up to chance is to do an injustice to those who give you the money in the first place, not to mention the people you serve.

THE ART AND SCIENCE OF FUNDRAISING

Fundraising is both the art of relationships and the science of planning and tracking.

Really, when it comes down to it, as someone raising money for your nonprofit, you must be able to inspire people to give to your organization (instead of giving to the other one), and then show them through excellent systems that you've made good on your promises about how the money will be spent.

Which means, to be really good at fundraising, you need to understand both sides: the art of sales and the science of systems.

Everyone is better at one than the other. As you find yourself focusing on one side of the coin, you need to supplement your skills to get the other side done as well. Expand your own skill set, and consider bringing in staff and board members to help.

Chapter 28

DONOR ENGAGEMENT

Learning how to engage donors—how to speak in a way that will inspire them to take action on behalf of your cause—is a critically important skill, one that will be used in every single fundraising effort in your organization.

I pause here to say that this section pertains to every facet of fundraising. Nothing will happen—your events won't be successful, you'll blow the site visit, you won't make your annual giving budget, you won't achieve the goals of your capital campaign—if you don't engage donors.

While this book doesn't delve into specific details around every donor giving strategy—such as planned giving, capital campaigns, and annual giving techniques (which would each take an entire book on its own)—I will say this: If you don't get donors to look you in the eye, if you don't get them to buy into what you are saying— what you are selling—then none of these development strategies will succeed. So the big question, of course, is how?

How do you engage donors effectively? How do you get them to give to your cause?

It starts with you.

It starts with your passion. It starts with your ability to show energy for the cause—*your* cause—which needs money.

This kind of energy can truly show only when you ask for money for a cause you care about. It sounds obvious, but I know plenty of people who have taken on a management level role at a nonprofit whose mission wasn't especially inspiring to them. Perhaps they needed a job or wanted to get out of their current one. Perhaps they were looking to move up and found the title they were looking for, but at an organization for which they were somewhat ambivalent.

And while all of those reasons make sense professionally, the sales part of the fundraising pitch can be a whole lot more difficult if you can't speak passionately about why it is so important.

Don't think you can fake this. Your lack of authenticity will be obvious to the donor.

Once you've found a cause you care so much about that you're willing to spend your valuable time engaging others to give to it, the next challenge is, of course, figuring out how to do it.

Donor engagement is about building relationships, a skill that comes quite naturally for some.

These people love to do it. They can strike up a conversation with anybody. They are unafraid to have deep conversations. They don't tell bad jokes. They read body language and respond accordingly. They are intuitive and confident in the moment, able to take the temperature of the conversation as it progresses and move it in a meaningful direction.

These individuals were born with a gift—a somewhat rare one. Find someone who can do this *and* ask for money and you've found a member of a very, very small minority of people.

For the rest of us not born with the knack of engagement, there are plenty of ways to develop this skill if we are willing to put the time and energy into learning and practicing it. It won't necessarily cause a personality shift. It won't necessarily make you like engaging donors more. It may, however, help you successfully get the gifts your organization needs.

Ten Tips to Successful Donor Engagement

And so I offer the following ten tips as a starting place for donor engagement. These apply to new donor prospects, but also to current donors who you are trying to get to give even more.

A note before we begin: These tips might seem quite simple, especially to those who have been soliciting donations for a while. But I have to say that I am often extremely surprised by how often organizations—including their development staff, their EDs, and their board members—fail to either recognize these principles or put them into practice.

Don't let this be the case. The money will not come if you don't get donors to give it to you.

And your organization will not succeed.

Tip 1. Do your homework.

Before you meet with prospective donors, do some homework. Everyone has a reason for his or her connection to your organization. What is theirs? Try to find out.

Find out what their interests are, and what other nonprofits they've been involved in. Find out what they do for a living, and if they have kids. You'll start way ahead of the game if you can speak to their passions, interests, and life experiences. And these days there are far too many ways to get some simple background on people, so there are no excuses to show up cold.

Tip 2. Be natural.

Now that you've got the meeting scheduled and done your homework, it's time to engage. To give yourself the greatest chances of a positive outcome, you need to do one thing at that meeting—right from the word *go*:

Put the person at ease.

It's critical that you start the meeting off right, and putting the person at ease is how to do it. It means making your conversation natural, not forced. It means talking to current or potential donors as *people* first, not as the donors in the database whose money you desperately need to help you make budget. Your budget crisis is not their problem.

Start by letting them know that you do want to talk about the very latest updates at your organization and a variety of ways they might get involved. But tell them you first want to hear about them (more on this starting with tip 3). And be sincere.

Keep them engaged and be authentic. Be natural.

If for any reason the situation feels awkward, donors will find an excuse to bolt. Quickly. Or, if they are just too nice, they'll stick the meeting through but it will be torture for them. And chances are there will be no gift in the end.

You need to be present, focused, and charming, and to show the donor that you are happy to be there.

Having a hard time getting traction on this? Read on.

Tip 3. Ask questions.

If you're doing your best to get things going and there's not any kind of click, don't panic. It's time to implement one of the best, most effective tools there is to engage donors—or anyone, for that matter.

Ask them questions.

We all have a lifetime of experiences and wisdom that we bring to each and every table. It's your job to get the person on the other side to talk about what makes him or her unique, and to show that you're interested.

To be clear, the questions you ask aren't about the person's connection to the organization or how he or she can support it. Not yet. These first questions are about getting to know donors on a more personal level, about getting them to open up, about putting them at ease.

What kinds of questions should you ask? I find I can always fall back on a few good ones:

• *"How are things at the office?"*

I ask them about their day-to-day job. I ask them how long they've been doing it. I ask them about their experiences in their particular field. I ask them why they chose it.

When I do this, I genuinely try to learn something I didn't know before about an occupation. That's engagement.

- *"Where did you grow up?"*

I try to learn about their personal histories. Whether they were born in this very town or a winding path led them to it, there are stories to tell and questions that will draw the stories out. Ask about their interests and hobbies. Donors are more than dollars in their wallets. Treat them like it.

- *"What is your opinion about…?"*

People love to share their opinions about all kinds of things.

You can ask them about the big news story of the week. You can ask them how they're handling the recent weather, or what they think of the latest singer or actor to enter rehab. Just get them talking, and then listen.

As things loosen up, the questions can turn to their experiences with the nonprofit sector, and where they think the greatest needs are. That will lead you into questions that get at why they care about your organization and what it does. (If you've done your homework, you should already have some kind of answer to this.) Once you get them engaged with the needs of the community and your organization, it's an easier transition to the rest of the conversation.

One caveat on seeking opinions: Be careful about discussing politics, religion, or anything else that might be volatile. If you don't know that you are absolutely in sync on these things, don't go there. There are plenty of other things to talk about.

The key point here? To effectively engage donors, you need to be genuinely interested in other people and what their life experiences are. If you truly don't care, you're in the wrong business. You can fake it for only so long before people know it.

Tip 4. Don't talk about yourself.

One of the biggest mistakes I see is for people to think that engaging someone starts by talking about themselves.

Resist this temptation. This is not about you.

Yes, a conversation is a two-way street, but in this scenario you are much more of a listener than a talker. You are asking questions to show that you are genuinely interested and want to learn about the other person's interests and passions.

Do not think you are getting donors to engage in a dialogue about their families by talking about yours first. And do not talk too long at any one time.

Become obsessed with noting nonverbal cues. If you're talking too much it will be obvious. Listeners will pull up their shirtsleeves to glance at their watch. Their eyes will drift to other parts of the room. Their face will begin to look a bit blank, as thoughts about their next meeting or that evening's favorite TV show begin to creep in.

When this happens, wrap up whatever you're talking about and get the focus back on them.

Tip 5. Know that your work is sales.
Sales doesn't have the greatest reputation, and that's especially true in the nonprofit sector. The mere word makes many of us think of inauthentic pitches for time shares and men's suits.

These are, indeed, a type of sales. *Bad* sales.

But there is such a thing as *good* sales, and that's when it has to do with meaningful products and services. Like those offered through your nonprofit, which advance your very important mission in some way.

When you, as part of your organization, engage in fundraising, you engage in sales. Good sales. The money you bring in goes toward a cause that matters. You need to understand and embrace this.

If you are unwilling to believe your job is sales, if you think this is an organic process, one where the prospects merely need to hear about your great work and will hand over their hard-earned money, you are kidding yourself.

If you build it, they will come is a fallacy. Remember, there are plenty of great causes out there competing for donor attention. Your job as a fundraiser is to convince people to give their dollars to *you*.

How do you do this? By getting to know them and building relationships. By going deeper. When I met with a potential donor I wasn't the "CAP ED." I was Deirdre, and they trusted and liked me. Then they gave to me on behalf of my organization.

This didn't happen because I was the most charming person in the room or the best salesperson in town. This happened because I engaged them effectively as people.

Think about effective salespeople you know. Remember how a positive sales experience got you to act in the way the salesperson wanted you to. Then analyze it in your mind, figure out how the person did it, and emulate it.

Fundraising is sales. If you can't face it, don't be in the business. A final word on this point...

Sales does not mean pressure. High-pressure pitches are *bad* sales. You don't need to spin. You are convincing someone to give to you because you are doing great work and there is hope for an even greater future at your organization.

If you are in a crisis, don't obsess on that point. Be transparent about why you need the money now, but don't play the victim or tell people you'll fold if they don't step up. This is not their problem.

And besides, who wants to invest in something that could fail tomorrow?

Tip 6. Remember that you're not asking for rent money.

If that last tip created a creeping taste of bile in your mouth, know that this response is natural in the beginning. Embracing that you're a salesperson, when so many of us look with contempt on the word, can be hard at first.

Let me assure you that engaging in sales for a nonprofit is a pure, authentic, wonderful endeavor. You are not asking for money for you. You are not asking someone to buy a product that person may or may not need.

You are asking people to pay for services that are critical to your community. And you know this because you believe heartily in your mission.

Asking for money for your organization is not akin to when you were a child and wanted more allowance. You are performing the service of acting as a transactional (but relational) intermediary on behalf of a nonprofit you believe in.

Now, swallow hard, remember this, and practice.

Still having a hard time with the actual ask? See page 175.

Tip 7. Be on time.

Okay, now to the nitty and gritty, and what seems like the most obvious of points.

Trust me…I'm including this tip for a reason. Because far, far too many people don't do it. And this can put the gift in jeopardy—rightfully so, because there's absolutely no excuse for it.

Show up at your meeting before the donor. Organize your day and your tasks to make it happen.

Donor engagement relies on proving that you believe a person's time, information, and dollars are valuable. Don't blow it by showing the person that other, more important things have taken precedence.

Tip 8. Turn off any and all hand-held devices.

This is another obvious tip, and another one I've seen disregarded.

Know this: No matter how sly you think you're being by subtly checking emails under the table or choosing to listen to a voicemail message while your potential donors are reviewing some information, they are on to you. And it shows them they are not worth your complete focus. That they are not as valuable as you've said they are.

You must be present. You must focus solely on them. You must resist the temptation to do anything but prove to them that they are your very first priority at this very moment.

It's a cliché because it's true: Actions really do speak a whole lot louder than words.

Tip 9. Follow up.

Unless it's the very last meeting at the very end of the day, the second you return to your office, send the donors a note thanking them for their time and interest, and telling them how much you appreciated the conversation. Email is fine to start. Following up with a written note is even better.

And if you made any promises, deliver them as quickly as you can.

- If you committed to sending them additional information, send it to them.
- If you told them you'd connect them with another person, do it.
- If you promised you'd provide them with the name and number of your kids' pediatrician so they could find one for their own kids, provide it.

Want people to feel special? *Show* that they've got your attention. Show that you meant what you said during your meeting.

Want to botch up your carefully crafted donor engagement program? Fail to follow up. It won't just relay the message that you weren't being completely honest when you told the potential donors they are a priority, but it also gives the impression that you aren't good for your word, which could extend to how you use their money.

This simple misstep could easily undo all of that hard work from tips 1 through 8.

Tip 10. Don't chew gum.

Okay, this one is admittedly a bias for me, but since I have your attention (and it's my book), I'm going to say it anyway.

Don't. Chew. Gum.

I promise you I did not include this because I couldn't come up with a tenth tip. I really mean it.

As is the case with many issues, I think this one comes to me quite naturally through my upbringing. My father, who by the way was an incredible salesman, *hated* gum chewing. He hated the sight of it. He hated the sound of it. He hated the smell of it.

I say it again. He was an incredible salesman.

Perhaps the two aren't related. Plenty of people chew gum and it's absolutely fine. You have every right to do so.

But...

When you're trying to engage donors, when you're asking meaningful questions, when you're putting your everything into showing them how interested you are in what they have to say, gum chewing is distracting at best. Plus, if you haven't mastered how to do it with your mouth closed, it's pretty gross to watch.

If you are a gum chewer, throw it away before you enter the meeting. There will always be a new piece waiting for you when you're done.

Chapter 29

THE ASK

I talked about it in the previous section. I talked about it in the boards section. It's an ongoing discussion in every nonprofit, in every fundraising circle.

You could do everything right. You could set up the right kind of meeting and have the perfect fundraising plan, but in the end, at some point, you need to be able to ask for money.

For most, the hardest, most stressful, greatest "ick" part of all is the question itself, which can get stuck right there in your throat.

"Are you willing to give us money today?"

Why is this so hard? Because asking for money is incredibly difficult.

Money is a sticky topic for many of us in general. Most of us were brought up with all kinds of ideas about where it does and does not belong in a conversation.

It's awkward. Awkward when we divide up the check at lunch. Awkward when we talk about it with our families. Awkward when a check bounces. Awkward when someone notices the make of our car, the size of our home, the label on our clothes. It becomes a value, akin to our worth.

No matter what, I can say definitively, again, that I have met very few people in my career who have the stomach to ask the question without any hesitation. For the rest of us, it takes a whole lot of planning and a good dose of practice.

Even then it's not easy. You can practice all you want but when it comes down to dialing that number, chances are you still might pray, pray, pray that it goes to voicemail so that you have an excuse to avoid the ask.

Know that you are far from alone. But also know that there really is no true excuse. You need to learn to ask for money. The people you serve are counting on you.

The best way to get yourself to do it, then get good at it? First, remember.

- Remember that you are acting as an ambassador for an organization and a cause that is important to you.
- Remember that this organization needs money to get the mission done effectively.
- Remember the people you serve.
- Remember your commitment to whatever role you signed up for that put you in this position.
- Remember that you are not asking for money for yourself; you are asking for money to help a cause, to advance a community.

Think back to those times you have had to spit out words you hated. Whether you were calling someone on an uncomfortable situation or you had to deliver bad news, remember that you felt lousy about it, but you did it.

You did it. And you can do it again.

Remember, and then practice.

- Practice asking the question. Do it aloud.
- Then practice asking the question and shutting up while you wait for a reply.
- Practice not making an apologetic face or letting the other person off the hook if things get awkward.
- Practice with others who have to do it, too.

Know that you will hear the word "no" a lot. And that's okay. This isn't personal. You are doing your job.

You will only be able to do this if you make up your mind to do so.

And you'll get better at it over time. I promise.

Chapter 30

GETTING CORPORATIONS ON YOUR SIDE

Requesting money from a corporation—one that involves a potential sponsorship or partnership—also involves an ask. But there's a marked difference.

It ain't all about altruism.

When companies partner with you, they are getting something—something more than feeling good—in return. Your job is to help them understand that return on investment.

You are dedicated to a specific mission that impacts a specific group of people, and you have a group of stakeholders who make it their business to support you. You reach passionate, loyal audiences that corporations also want to reach—audiences that will be introduced to and buy their products. Audiences that will become loyal to them.

By connecting with you, companies not only illustrate their commitment to being socially responsible, but they do so in front of a whole lot of people they want to reach, people who will help them make their own bottom lines.

When you approach corporations about a partnership, you come from a position of strength. You have something to offer, so know it up front. And use it.

Sure, people who work in corporations care about your cause. But the world is not about pure altruism. People want something for what they are giving, and you have it.

The trick now is to convince them.

To do so...

- First get clear on the value you bring. Explicitly identify how aligning with you brings in the exposure, audiences, and loyalty they are looking for. Help companies understand who your stakeholders are, how passionate they are, and why their loyalty to you might translate into loyalty to them.

- Put this all, succinctly, into a packet of information, one that outlines the impact of your programs on the clients you serve and then emphasizes statistically who you reach—from a donor perspective, a community stake-holder perspective, and a business perspective.

- Put that value you bring into numbers. What is it worth if a company's logo appears next to yours on a banner, in an ad, or on your website? They need to pay you for it. If you're stuck on defining an actual amount, look at similar-sized organizations and see how they value themselves. Adapt it to your own organization. Don't sell yourself short on this. Think in the thousands of dollars when creating this value statement, not the hundreds. Companies need to show consumers that they care, that they are committed to making this world a better place, that they have a mission, too. They get a lot for their dollar when they get to align with you.

- Include a number of partnership options, such as different sponsorship levels at an event, so that companies will feel some flexibility in how they can work with you. Make sure that you create enough incentive for them to aim high in their partnership with you.

Note that I used the word invest above. This is not a donation. This is a professional business decision on their part, one where they are putting money in to get something out. Make sure you treat it the same way.

Go to them and beg, and they will have all the power. Explain why you can get them what they want, and watch the tables turn.

Once you establish this partnership, honor it. Treat it like gold. It's easier to *reengage* someone who already values you than to engage someone new from scratch.

Chapter 31

EVENTS

I'm not going to sugarcoat this. Between my ED role, my board tasks, and my time with fundraising associations, I've been involved in just about every kind of fundraising strategy. And here's what I've come to know about myself.

I hate events.

I hate them for all kinds of reasons.

Part of it is that I'm a total, unadulterated forest person. (See page 122.) I am all about the big picture. The bigger, the better.

Forest people have a hard time with events because to do them well, you've got to be really good at details. You have to be on top of getting permits and know how to put together seating charts. You have to attend menu tastings and talk about décor. You have to pay special attention to who is on your RSVP list and which vendors require what kinds of insurance.

These are all important and will make or break the experience at a fundraising event, not to mention whether or not it makes budget. I hate them all.

Another reason I hate events is because they are expensive. People—boards especially—don't always think about this when they have their big brainstorm about balancing the budget by throwing some kind of concert, one they are just positive everyone will want to attend.

As I write this, I'm working with an ED whose board thinks it would be "fun" to put on a golf tournament. They have no idea what greens fees and catering and marketing all cost. They don't understand the risk that comes with it—the risk that people won't show, that money won't be raised. They don't understand the intensive time, strategy, and effort that go into mitigating that risk. They just like to golf. And, after all, other organizations do it. And it sounds like a good idea. And they're the board and they get to have a say.

That say can lead to big money problems.

Before moving on, I do need so say that some events really do make sense for an organization. They make good money and secure great exposure. I'm not out to vilify all events, even if I personally hate them. I know that sometimes they are worth it.

But...

Just like everything else, events should never be taken lightly or for granted. Just because an event is a fun party doesn't mean it's fun to *plan*.

Whether you're considering a new event or one that you've held for years, the most important thing you can do is take a good look at your resources, the money you will feasibly bring in (it's probably less than you're thinking), the money it will realistically cost (it's probably more than you're thinking), and the value-added benefits (exposure, media coverage, the opportunity to honor those who have contributed to your organization, etc.). Then, when all is on paper and weighed out, decide if holding that event—again or for the first time—really makes sense. Just know that virtually every other kind of fundraising initiative will cost you less to do, so make sure it's worth it.

And know this: Justifying a fundraiser that doesn't hit budget but is a good time is not an excuse to have it—or have it again.

One of CAP's biggest fundraising events was our annual art auction. It took a ton of time, a ton of energy, and a ton of work.

One year, it didn't hit budget. In fact, it came in far under. "But," the development director said upon giving me the news, "there is a bright side. It was a fantastic event. Everybody is talking about what a great time they had."

I looked at him and said, as nicely as I could, "And that would be fine if the mission of our organization is to put on great events. But it's not. It's to help people with AIDS."

LEARN FROM ME: HOW I MESSED UP SOME EVENTS AND LEARNED TO PUT ON SUCCESSFUL ONES

One other reason I have such a strong negative reaction to events is because of the trauma I experienced thanks to the biggest one we put on every year. The granddaddy of them all. The one that took up a big chunk of our budget. The one that stressed me out each and every time.

The event was AIDS Walk Colorado, the largest AIDS fundraiser in the state. My organization spent all year planning for it. It was a touching day, a day filled with celebrations and awareness building. And, in its heyday, it made a ton of money. In fact, before my time at the organization, when AIDS was *the thing* to support, AIDS Walk Colorado made millions.

But by the time I arrived on the scene, after AIDS faded from the spotlight as *the* cause to support, the walk wasn't such an easy sell for potential participants. And the ever-decreasing annual revenue reflected it.

Every year we tried to get it back up. We pushed and pushed, fried out our staff, tried every creative incentive we could think of to get people involved. And in the end, despite all of the pushing, it didn't matter. Of the seven AIDS Walks that happened on my watch, one actually made what it was supposed to make.

One.

I hated the walk.

This is quite ironic, really, because it was an incredible day. It was a day of inspiration and remembrance. It was a day where thousands of people came together to proclaim they were not going to let the cause go away. And as the day approached, I would talk it up to anybody who would listen—to staff, board, volunteers, the media. I would tell them how special it was, how important it was, how we loved it.

But then, every year on walk day I'd get up before dawn and get ready to make my way to the park. Every year, before I got there, I'd stop at the same Burger King and get physically sick in the same restroom because I just couldn't handle the stress. Every year I smiled and thanked people and hooted and hollered for the full ten kilometers. And every year I'd make my way back to the office after it was all over, as the finance person added up the deposit slips and projected the bottom line. Every year I'd sit in my office and wait for the news.

And every year but one, the news was bad.

It seemed that no matter how low we set the budget or how realistic, creative, and innovative we tried to be, it didn't matter. Every year we came up short. And every year I had to then adjust the budget to make up for it. Which meant, every year, I had to make cuts.

The AIDS Walk truly was a meaningful experience for those who weren't responsible for the money it raised—and those who didn't rely on it. For those of us who did, it was a painful way to learn some valuable lessons about fundraising events.

Allow me to name a few. Perhaps they will spare you some pain.

Lesson 1: Don't create an event to help you solve your budget problem.

As I mentioned above, nonprofits—particularly board members—love events. Part of it is that it's a fundraising strategy that we can all understand. Many of us were brought up around bake sales and carnival days and black-tie affairs, all in the name of raising money. We *get* how fundraising events work. We can wrap our heads around them.

Events are also beloved because they are an easier sell. At an event, people are getting something for their money—such as art, a chance to honor a community member, or a meaningful experience.

I've seen lots of well-intended people come up with special event ideas that they truly believe *can't lose*. They are just absolutely certain that people will come out in swarms for them. (Who doesn't love another black-tie gala? Plenty!) Or maybe they believe they're getting the deal of a lifetime. (We'll have to pay for the venue but they'll throw in the catering!) Or maybe they believe that if they build it, the people will just come. (A fallacy, see page 171.)

The truth of, course, is that many, many events lose money. And sometimes, if you've measured your risk, if the event has potential, if you'll be okay even if it bombs, that risk is still worth it.

But far too often, especially around budget time, when board and staff members look at that gaping hole between the revenue the organization is supposed to be bringing in and what's actually arrived, an event feels like the perfect fix.

Chances are it won't be.

Lesson 2: Be realistic.
We tried. We tried so hard. My first few years, the AIDS Walk hovered at about $850,000 gross. Then we slipped to $750,000. Then to $650,000.

Why? Because, as I've said, AIDS wasn't the name of the game anymore.

Each year at budget time we added the walk to our budget. And every year we put as our projection the same amount we'd raised the year before. If we did it once, we convinced ourselves, we could do it again.

And every year we were kidding ourselves. Because every year it was more apparent that support for our cause was slipping. And every year, when we set our revenue goal, I knew deep down I should cut it low—lower than ever before. But I didn't. I needed to balance my organizational budget, and this felt like a great way to do it. And so I'd put off the inevitable and suffer as a result. Because soon after that fateful walk day—usually the day right after the event—I had to swallow hard, gather my executive team together, and readjust for the year. Which meant making cuts—usually around $100,000. Money that we didn't have.

The lesson? Budget feasibly, and be brutally honest. And, when it's all over, take a good, long look in the event-planning mirror and learn from your mistakes. Where you spent too much. Where you missed an opportunity. And—this one stings—whether or not it really made sense to have the event in the first place.

Lesson 3: Know when you're making budget because of dumb luck or circumstances beyond your control.

- If you put on a golf tournament and there's a golf-loving donor paying all the expenses, be clear that this is the precise reason you made budget.
- If you've got a corporate sponsor that gives you six figures to cover a concert, and the business goes under, know that you are in trouble.
- If a staff member is best friends with a theater owner and you make all kinds of money from a benefit show, know that the money goes away when the staff member goes away.

Sometimes you make budget because of hard work, careful strategy, and determination. Sometimes it has nothing to do with you. Be aware of the difference, and don't think you can just pull everyone up by the bootstraps and get it done if you can't.

Lesson 4: Know when to say when.

We come up with all kinds of reasons to hold events:

- The community loves them, and so do we.
- They are a part of our history.
- They get us exposure.
- They engage people.
- They convert the public into donors.

These are all important. But at the same time, you need to think about the absolute, primary reason for this event.

If it's a fundraising event, chances are that first and foremost it needs to make money. Probably a lot of it. If this is the case, own it. And use that knowledge to make your decisions.

How much is the exposure helping you, really? Are you really increasing donors as a result, and by how much? Will community members boycott you if the event goes away?

Events, just like everything else, serve their purpose. After a time, some no longer really have one. Look objectively at your events and make the right decision for the right reasons.

The right reason, by the way, is almost never "Because we've always done it this way."

Lesson 5: Know how much an event really costs you.
Remember the art auction? (See page 180.)

The art auction budget included costs for the logistics, the printing, and the food for meetings. It did not, however, include the cost for the fundraising staff. It didn't include any portions of other impacted salaries, such as those of our marketing person or our development director, or me for that matter.

We tend to overlook these expenses because they are a part of our organization's budget. And so we think these expenses are already paid for.

But the truth is that all resources, including our human ones, are finite. Spending them down on events that aren't successful is a wasted opportunity, because they could be used for new strategies, more cost-effective ones—perhaps for prospecting. Perhaps, even, for planning better events.

When you make your decisions about having or continuing an event, analyze what it will really cost you—every penny—not to mention the energy, the time, and the level of frustration. It all counts.

Chapter 32

GRANTS

I've often been asked about the keys to getting grants. This question I can answer with particular authority because my organization was heavily grant funded, both privately and through the government, and I was involved in a lot of grant management.

Grants management includes a wide variety of important components, each of which can lead to a grant program's success—or failure.

Because it was such a critical component of our revenue stream, I got to know the ins and outs of grants. I got to know what to do and, of course, what not to do. And, as always, I learned many of these things by doing them wrong the first time.

So save yourself some stress and learn from me.

Tips for Grants Management

As in other sections, some of the "don'ts" may seem obvious, but if I didn't commit these offenses myself, and see them committed all over the sector, I wouldn't be listing them here.

Tip 1. Don't apply for grants for which you're not eligible.
In concept, this one seems the most obvious of all. But for some reason when we get involved in an organization that we love so much, we tend to get blind to this one, especially if we're hurting for money and there's some on the table.

And so we see requests for proposals that clearly dictate that the organizational budget be under a million, and even though we're at

$5 million we apply anyway. We see that the funder provides grants for mental health research, but we put in a request for mental health counseling. We see that the board must reflect certain demographics, and we just skip over that question because we know ours doesn't.

And we think we'll get away with this.

And what happens? Not only do we *not* get the funding. Not only do we look extremely foolish to the frustrated group of people who have carefully thought through the grant requirements before releasing the grant application. We have also wasted a whole lot of time and energy.

If you think there is flexibility on some of the requirements, call and ask first. It's better to know up front and be realistic, no matter how much it might sting if you learn that you're wrong.

Tip 2. Answer the questions.
I've worked with a number of large foundations, and I've heard it over and over again: the frustration experienced by grant committees—each and every grant cycle—because the applying organizations failed to answer the questions.

Instead, the answer to a question about strategic goals focuses on an organization's fundraising goals. The answer to a question about the number of youth on the board actually reflects the number of youth on the staff (presumably because this number felt stronger). Or—and this one is very common—organizations skip some questions altogether, either because they don't have an answer, they don't have a *good* answer, or they get sloppy, get rushed, and miss the questions.

It's important to remember that there are people behind these grant applications, and they take their jobs seriously. They will not forget when you fail to honor their time and process. So don't.

Tip 3. Budget enough time to get it done. Then add more.
Grants need to be written carefully and strategically, with excellent word choice and correct grammar. They must be reviewed by the

right people on staff, and the application must contain all enclosures.

The best way to mess this up is to drop your grant off at 4:55 p.m. on the day it's due because you didn't start it until the day before.

We've all done it. I look back at one unfortunate car ride and wonder just how I didn't kill anybody on the road. We got the application there with literally 30 seconds to spare. Not only did it produce major amounts of stress for us, it also resulted in an application we weren't especially proud of, filled with all kinds of errors and sloppy language.

When you know you have a grant due, think about how long it will take, then calendar out your process: the meetings you'll need to have and the time it will take to write it, for all appropriate eyes to review it, and to coordinate the budget and the other appendices. Then, add 50 percent more time. You'll need it.

Tip 4. Work that site visit like nobody's business.

One of my favorite things to do, both as an ED and as a board member, is to participate in site visits. If you submit a grant and are lucky enough to have the opportunity to host someone from the funding organization at your nonprofit, use it as the prime opportunity that it is.

The great thing about site visits is that the hardest part is already done. Not only have you thought through your messages and made your arguments, not only do you already know that you're a match for the funder's priorities, you've also already done the part everyone dreads the most: you've asked for the exact amount of money. *And* you know they have it to give. All that's left is to get them to give it to you.

This is your greatest sales scenario—the pitch without the ask. I loved selling CAP to anyone who would listen, and I made sure we made that site visit as compelling as possible. We'd give them a tour and talk about our programs and their outcomes. We'd make the listeners laugh. We'd offer them food. We had program people on hand who could tell inspiring stories about our clients. Sometimes we'd have clients on hand as well. We charmed the funders. We were sincere about the great things we were doing with our organization. And, when it was all over, we'd thank them—both electronically and with a handwritten note.

We not only got them to believe in us and believe in our programs, we got them to like us.

Remember, grants are just another vehicle to reach a funder and foster a relationship. There are real, individual people behind funders, and they're coming to you. A site visit is another way to involve yourself in excellent donor engagement. (See page 165.) It's an opportunity to use your powers of persuasion to get a person to give to you instead of giving to the other guy. Nobody owes you anything, so this is your chance to give a funder a reason to believe in you, to be inspired by you.

Sometimes we'd work that site visit so well that the person would become our greatest ambassador, advocating on our behalf to the other decision makers at the funding organization. It doesn't get any better than that.

One other point on site visits: They are also a great way to get the board involved. Not only does it reflect well to have a board member in the room, it also helps the board member hear how good you are at selling your organization, and it teaches that person how to do the same. Win-win-win.

Tip 5. Do what you say you're going to do.
Far too often, nonprofits write grant applications and make all kinds of promises without being especially certain as to how they will pull them off.

I called a seasoned ED once to talk about partnering together on a grant application. Her exact words: "Let's just say we're going to collaborate. We'll figure out the details later."

It happens all the time. We write grants that require us to commit to programs and outcomes that aren't in place or haven't been defined. We say to ourselves thoughtfully, "Yeah, we can do that…," and then we get the money and six months later, when we have to turn in our first report, we realize there wasn't a *snowball's chance* we could do that.

How does this happen?

It's quite natural, really. Nonprofits need money. They need it badly and they need it now, and so when a grant looks like the right fit and they are on a deadline, they do their best to answer the questions. That's how it happens.

But it shouldn't. When you commit yourself to things you might not be able to pull off, you set yourself up for one of two things:

One, not doing it, then having to report this back to the funder and losing all kinds of credibility, making it virtually impossible to get any future money out of the foundation.

And two, not doing it, and then writing your progress report in a way that is ambiguous and flimsy instead of answering the questions in a professional, quantitative, and expected way. Then you skip the part about the commitments you made and how you're doing in meeting them altogether.

Let me tell you this.

The funders are on to you. They know. They see it all the time. No amount of creative writing can mask the fact that you made commitments you haven't kept.

So, as you write your grants and fill in the goals section, think through what you will really be able to pull off as a result of the funding. Be realistic. Be reasonable. Be feasible. Know that your staff and your organization will do its best every day, but also has limits. And know that new projects tweaked to fit into grant eligibility will take more time and more money to execute than you're thinking they will.

One final note on this point: Do not let your first reminder of what you're supposed to be achieving for a given grant happen because the first progress report is due. You and your staff should always know what you've committed to and be monitoring it over time.

Too often we get that wonderful letter, the one that tells us we've been funded, and then we breathe a sigh of relief, celebrate our success, and file it in a drawer until the next time we need to deal with it. Which is when we realize we haven't done all of the things we said we were going to do. Or any of them.

Wrong.

Celebrate, yes. But keep the file handy.

Tip 6. Know the truth about government grants.
Government grants were both my greatest blessing and my greatest curse at CAP.

They were a significant percentage of our funding. They brought in much-needed dollars and they made sure our programs were sustained. They were also based on legislation, which meant we knew they would continue for a while. Those were the good points.

At the same time, they were incredibly cumbersome. Many applications actually came with multiple, multilayered forms for different pots of money, each one accompanied by somewhat repetitive narrative requirements, tedious charts about outcomes, and budget templates that didn't relate to the real financial world in any way. The midyear and final reports were more of the same, only worse because we had to justify just how we spent all the money, and why our messy little nonprofit didn't fit quite so snugly into their clean, bureaucratic spreadsheets.

All of this was a tremendous pain, but we knew it from the beginning. We knew that by engaging in these government grants we were agreeing to a high level of tedium and inconvenience. And because we were clear on our cost-benefit analysis, because we knew we'd get significant dollars for our hardship, this was okay.

But there was one piece that wasn't okay, and it caused major anxiety for me.

The grants were reimbursed. Meaning we put out the cash, and then we got it later. Sometimes *much* later. Which left us in an incredibly precarious position.

There was a constant cash flow tug-of-war and a constant sinking feeling in the pit of my stomach, a constant mosquito nipping at the back of my brain, that we might not be able to make it through this month, that payroll might be in jeopardy.

One of my lowest moments as an ED came because of this issue—when hubby found me at 2:30 in the morning, sitting in my walk-in closet, working through a cash flow report.

Ick.

Reimbursed funding is very common in the government grants world. If you decide to jump into it, know this up front, strategize as best you can for cash flow challenges, and plan for some sleepless nights.

Chapter 33

THE BOARD AND ITS FUNDRAISING ROLE

This is one of the stickiest issues there is in the nonprofit world. In fact, one of the reasons it's so sticky is because it actually combines two, individually sticky topics: money and boards. Both are needed to make the organization function. And both involve tough dynamics, creating tension for everyone involved.

We've already explored board issues and how to address them in the management section (see page 48). I won't go into all of that again, except to say that following the tips in those pages about building the board system and engaging in effective board selection will only help you on this issue.

But this section, and I know this is why you landed here, is really about taking the two topics—money and boards—and tying them together into one, big tricky question: How do we get the board to fundraise effectively?

It always comes up. Whether I'm conducting a training on boards, holding a workshop on fundraising, or coaching EDs one-on-one, one or several of the following specific questions rise to the surface:

How do we get the board to:
- Give more money?
- Get their friends to give money?
- Know their role is about raising money?
- Become good at raising money?
- Actually be compliant with our give-or-get policy?

I tried. I tried to find the answers. I looked for the keys to effectively getting the board to fundraise.

I searched for the proverbial magic bullet. And, as you probably expect, the news on this front isn't great. Because there isn't one.

So now, the truth.

Brace yourself.

Board members, just like most of us, hate asking for money.

We've talked about the general population, and just how many people have the interest, skill, and stomach to actually make the ask for money (and then stop talking). Very, very few.

Why would this be any different for your board?

For some reason, we bring on board members and we believe they will be completely different from the rest of us—that they will not only get that they're supposed to fundraise, but that they'll embrace fundraising, enjoy it, and be good at it.

It makes no sense. In general, with the exception of a teeny group of people, humans really hate fundraising.

Boards? They're human, too.

So now that we've figured that out, now that we know that most board members (just like the rest of us) will not only hate asking for money but really won't be very good at it, we face the question: Where does this leave your board and its fundraising role? Shouldn't your board members learn *how* to be good at it? If they cared enough, wouldn't they put in the time to do this?

My answer may not be popular, but it's realistic, it's fair, and it will create significantly more peace in the life of the nonprofit executive:

No.

Do they care? Sure. But let's get real. Your board—or at least the majority of the people on it—will not be good at fundraising, specifically the asking part. So don't expect it.

This fact is hard to swallow. It doesn't feel right. We truly believe that boards should be great at fundraising, should do it often, should do it well, and, truth be told, should *like* it.

That's a tall order, not to mention unrealistic.

So I say the first thing *you* should do is accept this fact.

And it *is* a fact. Most things I write are subjective opinions. But not this one. Your board members won't like fundraising. Most won't be good at it. Most won't even try it.

But…

Let's be clear. What this *doesn't* mean is that boards get a free pass when it comes to doing their part to bring money into your organization.

- They need to understand the role fundraising plays for you, the kinds of dollars you need to raise, and how you plan to go about doing it. They then need to figure out the role they will play in getting the dollars in the door.

- They also need to understand that they are the organization's greatest ambassadors. They are volunteers illustrating their commitment to the organization by taking on its heaviest role—fiduciary accountability. After all, they believe so greatly in the mission that they are attending board meetings, approving budgets, and evaluating the executive director, all for *free*.

- They need to be proud of their role on the board, and let everyone know about it. They need to talk about it when they are out at dinner, or in their own offices. They need to do this—not because I'm *shoulding* on them right now, but because they are excited and inspired to be a part of your organization.

And you, as the organization's leader, need to help them feel that way.

It shouldn't be that hard, right? Because they joined for the mission, remember?

But that mission—that passion that drove them to the organization in the first place—is easy for board members to forget when the meetings are tedious or uninspired, when there are all kinds of tense financial issues to discuss, or when their own professional lives are in turmoil.

So make that excitement possible. Make their ambassadorship role clear. Get them inspired, then re-inspired.

- Have staff come to board meetings to talk about the impact of their programs.
- Have clients come in to talk about the difference your organization made in their lives.
- Bring in outside trainers to clarify the board's *governance* role, and emphasize why doing it well is so critical to the health and strength of the organization.
- Work with your chair to spread the message about the critical nature of the board. Then spread it again.
- Work with those you trust on the board to clarify its fundraising role and be concrete. What, exactly, are they expected to do? What are their options?
  - Is it enough to attend events and get others to do the same?
  - Does attending site visits count?
  - What about calling donors to thank them for a recent contribution?
  - What about actually making the ask (for those few who have it in them to do so)?
  - Be clear about the annual giving expectations of the board itself. (This is a must-do. Grantors, donors, and other stakeholders don't look too kindly on organizations with anything but 100 percent board giving. And they shouldn't.)

Remember that certain board members will be good at asking and good at selling, but most will not. So figure out the minimum you expect from your board and *explicitly communicate* these expectations to potential board members. Do not bring on new members and then expect them to just know they need to fundraise and how to do it. Even worse, don't lay the expectations on them for the first time during their initial board meeting or at an orientation.

It's not fair. Do it before they commit.

Set Them Up for Success

Once you've determined the board's fundraising role, set them up for success by training them on how to play it.

- Bring in fundraising experts to help the board learn how to talk about the organization and sell it to others.
- Identify those members who really shine at this (there will likely be just one or two) and talk to them about being your partner in donor asks.
- The rest? Use them in the traditional ways—at networking functions, site visits, getting people to events, giving of themselves, et cetera. It's not ideal, but it's reality.

You need to set your board and yourself up for success by clearly defining the board's role, training them to carry it out, and knowing where their strengths lie—or don't. Your policies need to reflect it all, as does the board's job description. And in there should also be the very specific give-or-get board policy. There should be no gray area as to who needs to be doing what to bring dollars to the organization.

So there you have it—the harsh, unpopular but true reality checks (at least in my experience) pertaining to boards and fundraising. At least now you know and can plan for them accordingly.

And now for two more...

Reality Check 1: Staff can't hold the board accountable to all of this.
In most organizations it's the executive director or the development director who holds the board accountable for its give-or-get donation and its fundraising responsibilities.

Bad idea.

Despite what people want to believe and what many board members themselves will tell you, the board/staff dynamic represents a huge power differential.

This particular group of volunteers has more power than anybody else in the organization. Together they are the big boss. Expecting the ED, development director, or another staff member to be the one calling them to talk about their as-of-yet unrealized donation is incredibly awkward for that staff member. It needs to be the board leadership—the chair, development committee chair, or someone else designated by one of them—who does this. And all of it—who monitors it, who follows up with members, and when it will all go down—should be determined in a policy ahead of time.

Reality Check 2: Board members won't give up the names of their friends. Hear this clearly. Board members are not likely to give up the names of their wealthy friends.

Did you hear it? Really?

Most of us spend a lifetime gathering a circle of people with whom to spend our time. We enjoy their company and we grow in our relationships, building trust over many years, and finding those rare people with whom we celebrate our successes and also go to in our vulnerable moments.

This circle is very important for many people—sacred for some. So to expect board members to give up the names and contact information of these people is actually asking a lot.

Yet we expect them to do so without any hesitation.

We say they *should*.

In fact, we often bring people onto the board because we know that they have rich friends and we just assume there will be no problem in asking them for money, to purchase tables at events, to leave a bequest.

Even worse, we bring these board members on without telling them this is a big reason as to why they're being recruited. Then they get on the board, and we tiptoe around the topic at one of the meetings.

You know that meeting. The one where the ED or the development director hands out a sheet of paper and asks everyone to list five contacts who might give. We tell them they don't even need to do the ask—just put down the information and we'll call the prospects ourselves. *Ta-da!*

I have never seen this work.

We get so frustrated by board members who don't "step up" by asking their friends to give. But when it comes down to it, I ask, how many of us would want to do this?

Really, picture your friends. And if you sit there indignantly and insist you'd ask them, *really* picture doing so. Picture doing it once, then twice, then again, which is what we expect of our board members. And picture asking for money for different causes as you switch up your organizational involvement.

Not so easy, is it?

If you do expect your board members to ask their colleagues for money, you need to have a specific policy around it and express the expectation to them before they join. If you find yourself hesitating to inform a board member of this kind of policy, perhaps that should tell you something.

If you have a board member who you know has a strong connection to a well-known philanthropist in the community, don't assume that member will be comfortable making an ask. Approach the member directly and check his or her comfort level. Together, figure out the best way to solicit the donor and how you can support the board member in doing so.

The board-fundraising dynamic is tricky. We begin messing it up the second we create unrealistic expectations, or fail to let people know what those expectations are.

So don't. Save yourself and your board the pain of the unspoken truth in the room.

Don't create a budget that balances only if the board comes through with some silly amount of money. Don't expect your board members to love fundraising or be good at it. Find those members who are, and support them in this task. Find solid ways to get the others engaged in fundraising strategies that fit their skill sets.

And be sure to thank them every step of the way. This is not easy stuff. Those who actually come through are to be congratulated—regularly.

Chapter 34

MANAGING THE MONEY

Bringing in the money is not easy. We've covered that. You know it. You've lived it.

Me too.

But when I first stepped into my ED role, the challenges around *getting* the money were nothing compared to the challenges around accounting for it.

Remember, I came from marketing. I was a words and pictures girl. I could write. I could talk. I could visualize. Numbers? Not so much. In fact, not at all.

But here's what I found out: The job of an ED is to be a generalist. You need to know a whole lot about a whole lot. It's about leading and managing. It's about the forest and the trees. It's about politics and policies, systems and selection. It's about managing the board, managing the staff, managing the projects, managing the money.

Managing the money.

What does this mean? It means that when the money comes in, you need to know what happens to it. You need to understand the process—how it flows through your organization, gets entered into your systems, and gets to the bank, and that it is spent as it was intended.

You do not need to know how to do all of this yourself. My financial/accounting software system remained elusive to me until my last day. But I did know how the budgeting process worked. I did know how the check got to the bank. And I did know how to read the reports.

While getting the right people in your organization to manage your finances is absolutely critical, it is not your excuse to blow this part off or think you don't have to focus on it.

I learned this the hard way. Your finance person (or *people*, if you're big enough and lucky enough) will know how to create the reports. This person will feed the budget numbers in. He or she will help strategize how to keep things balanced, and will know how to prove all of this to any donor, who has every right to ask.

But it is up to you to know how to read it all, how to know that it's functioning, and how to make sure your finance person is accurately accounting for everything—restricted and unrestricted funds, capital and operating, balance sheets and incomes statements and cash flow reports.

This is very difficult for those of us who don't possess accounting degrees. How do you hold someone accountable when you don't exactly know what he or she is doing with those tricky adding machines and accounting software programs?

You put together good job descriptions, you recruit carefully (using great references), and you know the basics of what you're looking for—proven ability in accounting, strategizing, and forecasting, and someone who's not afraid to plug the numbers in. Ideally you find someone who knows the nuances of *nonprofit* accounting. You want someone who can communicate, in some cases *translate*, those numbers. You want someone who will respond to questions with neither condescension nor defensiveness.

Yet even when you find this person, it is still up to you to know how to read the financial statements the person produces and ask questions. It's your job to hold the organization together. It is up to you to make sure it is strong, stable, and sustainable. That's what you signed up for.

Know that, just like everyone else, even the greatest finance person will make mistakes, and you need to know how to spot them.

You certainly don't want your board to spot them first.

If you don't know the basics of nonprofit accounting, take a class, or a few. I did. In fact, as I've mentioned, the timing and reason for the pursuit of my master's degree was because I knew that I needed training in this specific area. I knew the health of my organization, and the effectiveness of me as an ED, relied on it.

I took it seriously. I read that nonprofit accounting textbook cover to cover, and I asked hundreds of questions. In the end, I was able to troubleshoot, strategize, and partner with my finance team to create budgets and reports that were feasible for the organization. I was able to understand our 990 and have a relatively intelligent conversation with our auditors. That class made me a better ED.

In the end, it may have saved my organization...and my job.

For most of us, managing the money is one of the parts we hate. It doesn't matter. We need to do it anyway. We need to do it well. We need to bring on others to help us. And we need to make sure it's done accurately, transparently, and legally. Only then can we move on to all of the other stuff we like so much better.

PART FOUR

MARKETING

Chapter 35

WHAT MARKETING REALLY IS

Marketing has a stigma attached to it—and it's somewhat deserved.

Too often we think of clichéd creative types sitting around a table loaded with lattes, tossing pencils at the ceiling while coming up with catchy one-liners and patting each other on the back for their creative genius. (I've met a lot of marketers, and I can tell you this is sometimes—often—true.)

Then there's another marketing stigma, this one central to the nonprofit world.

Nonprofit managers know instinctively that marketing is important. The problem is that many cannot articulate why, which tends to send it way down on the priority list, as a less critical component to meeting organizational goals.

What Most People Think

In our minds, marketing is:

- Creative jewelry for your organization—fancy words and tag lines that turn heads but don't do much else.
- A luxury, a sign that you have money to spare, and the first thing to go when times get tough.
- Something your organization deserves to get pro bono.
- Something you can pull off with a decent Microsoft Word program and a good photocopier.

The Truth

Far too often, the words above define precisely what marketing is for an organization. Which is why there's that stigma, because it doesn't really *do* anything.

But...

When done correctly, marketing *does* play a critical role. It *does* help you meet your organizational goals.

The truth is, marketing:

- Is a critical tool to your nonprofit's success in meeting its fundraising and programmatic goals.
- Requires strategic thought and careful consideration of return on investment before any kind of implementation should happen.
- Is every bit a science as an art.

The Good News

It is possible to do marketing well. Once you grasp the basics, get some expertise, and do a bit of research, you can make an exponential impact on your mission and therefore on those you serve.

Do it well and do it strategically, and your stakeholders will be inspired.

And they will act.

And your organization wins.

Chapter 36

MARKETING STRATEGY

I begin this section with the elusive definition of marketing. It's one I've created over time, one that gets to the heart of what marketing really does - what it's supposed to do, anyway.

Marketing inspires people to act on behalf of your organization to help reach its goals.

Each word in this definition was chosen carefully and deliberately. Marketing is not just meant to inform, but to *inspire action* that will work toward a predetermined purpose.

So now that you know what marketing *does*, let's talk about what marketing *is*.

I will say before I begin that there are differing opinions on this, but over time I've found this one to resonate the most with me and those I work with.

Marketing is the broad term to include all of the different ways you reach certain people (markets) with specific, targeted messages to inspire them to act in a way that reaches your organizational goals.

Imagine an umbrella. Underneath it are all of the strategies you use to reach your markets. These include media/public relations, outreach, social media, and advertising.

Each of these methods of reaching people, which I refer to as vehicles because they drive toward a certain audience, could be used at your organization—as long as you believe they will effectively get to your markets and inspire them to act.

- You might want to let everyone in town know about your upcoming fundraising walk, and so you use the media to broadcast it.
- You might want to recruit new women for your program, so you attend another organization's regularly scheduled women's group and talk to them directly, giving them meaningful information that they can take with them.
- You might want to get current donors to give again, and so you send them a targeted email that specifically thanks them for their gift and talks about how to continue their meaningful support.

These are all marketing strategies. It's not just about using the media or creating great materials. It's about:

- Recognizing your organizational goals and determining who will help you reach them. (These may be different sets of people for different goals.)
- *Then* figuring out where they are (in groups or as part of associations? Somewhere specific geographically? Represented in the broad audience?).
- *Then* figuring out which vehicle will get to them (media, outreach, hard copy, digital).
- *Then* writing a message that will get them to do what you want them to do, and tailoring it to that vehicle.
- *Then* getting it out there.
- *Then* reflecting on how successful it was after it's over, in part by asking your target market if they think it was, and adjusting your strategy accordingly.

To be clear, this M is about all of marketing, the whole kit and caboodle. It includes broad media relations and collateral material and websites. It includes social media and annual reports and outreach to specific audiences.

Marketing is not simply a press release or a fact sheet. It includes thinking through when it's time to appeal to a broad audience and when it makes sense to stick with your known champions. It is a comprehensive strategy. Do not throw tons of ideas and strategies against that proverbial wall to see what sticks. Do not waste your time or your marketer's time—or your organization's resources.

Just like everything else, marketing should be a strategic, intentional part of your overall organizational goals. Too often, marketing happens in a vacuum—a fun little brochure here, a flyer there, perhaps a blog thrown in for good measure (because, after all, everybody's doing it). When that happens, then marketing does indeed feel dispensable—and probably is.

Just like the money M and its fundraising plan, marketing must closely follow the organizational plan. Everything that happens on the marketing front needs to be done with the purpose of reaching a goal. Whether it is part of the programmatic strategy or part of the fundraising plan, every single marketing effort must feed into a greater purpose.

Despite what some organizations (and, famously, their boards) think, marketing is *not* about putting together a press release and sending it out every week. Marketing is *not* about a random 30 seconds on television that doesn't really say anything about you or what you need as an organization. It is *not* about a newsletter that talks about how great the staff is, or a Twitter account that proclaims it's office clean-up day.

I say it again: Marketing is about inspiring people to act in a way that drives your mission forward. Period.

Which means every single piece of marketing should be part of a greater strategy. It should get people to your events, inspire them for a future ask, or recruit people into a new program. Every piece of collateral or electronic real estate should target a specific audience, for a specific purpose, and a specific *ask*.

Do not forget this last part. Marketing must reflect what you need. Then it must ask for help in a compelling way—most often with the goal of getting contributions of money and time. It must ask people to give up a portion of their day, to give to you, attend one of your functions, or participate in your program.

Nobody owes you anything. We talked about this unpopular fact in the Money section (see page 161). Because of it, you must explain to people why they need to care about you. You must *inspire* them to act, not just on behalf of your organization, but *instead of* another organization that is also reaching out to them. You must show that you are not just worthy, but *the most* worthy of their time, their attention, and their dollars.

Easy, right? No. If it were easy, nonprofit marketers wouldn't be out of work all over town and people outside of your organization would have a better sense of what you do and why they should give to you.

LEARN FROM ME: HOW I LEARNED WHAT MARKETING REALLY IS

I'm going to be completely honest.

When I got my first job in marketing, I didn't know a thing about it. To be *completely* honest, I got that first title—public affairs/marketing associate—and didn't even really know the difference between the two. I knew marketing related to the materials we used to sell the organization, and that public relations played into it on the media end. But I didn't know how it all worked together—or how to develop strategies to make our work successful.

I was brought on because I'd worked in media and knew that world, and so I could help achieve our public relations goals. The rest, I reasoned, I'd just figure out.

And so I focused on the media relations piece, which is exactly what my boss, who considered himself a marketing expert (and was), wanted me to do.

Now, PR was easy. I knew the media game. I'd lived the media game. I knew who to call and I knew how to write a press release, and within a few weeks of my arrival at the organization I got some mainstream media attention at one of our events. For me, it was easy. Not because I was super smart, but because I'd lived it, because I knew my goals, and because I knew what I brought to the table that nobody else did.

The marketing skills came next. My boss was an extremely splashy kind of marketer. He walked around with poster boards of concepts and loved to play with visuals. He was all about the pictures. Words, on the other hand, weren't necessarily his thing, but they were mine. The partnership was perfect.

I learned everything I could from him, not even realizing, frankly, just how much I needed to learn.

It was only when he left five months later, when I took over the department, that I got it. I realized that marketing was our way of reaching our audiences, not just to look good or pat ourselves on the back, but to reach our organizational goals.

That's where things had fallen down. Our department had been doing great stuff—beautiful pieces and innovative designs. But we never talked about how all of this great stuff met any organizational goals. To be honest, I didn't even know what those organizational goals were.

This is extremely common—and exactly the reason why marketing is often seen as useless. It is why it's the first thing cut from organizational budgets. It is why marketing feels just so...dispensable.

Because it often is.

After I took over the department, after I realized that my job wasn't to make pretty things but to make pretty things that *did something*, I became a marketer. For real.

And now I'm a marketing instructor. Again, not because I'm all that smart, but because I know how to reach people. I know how to use marketing to inspire people to act in a specific way, toward specific goals. I know that it takes more than a cool piece of art or fun web-page animation to get people to put themselves out for your organization. To give to it. To volunteer for it. To act on its behalf.

Chapter 37

THE MARKETING PLAN

Now that you've got this down, it's time to put it in writing through a marketing plan.

It's easier to wrap your head around a fundraising plan. (See page 163.) After all, it's a quantitative thing, and you have a set number of categories clearly outlined in your budget that spell out your fundraising initiatives and their respective goals.

But marketing is creative and messy and wonderfully artistic, you think. It's not possible to take all of that ambivalent creativity and nail it down in a plan, right?

Wrong.

Marketing is strategic. Marketing forces you to think about your goals, and the audience who is going to help you reach those goals by acting in a certain way.

Every goal, whether programmatic or fundraising, should at least have some strategy for marketing, and for how collateral materials, good messages, and reaching the right audiences will drive the goal forward.

Like the fundraising plan, a marketing plan should include:
- The organizational goal (programmatic and fundraising), and the marketing goals that accompany it.
- The market you want to reach because it is most likely to act on your behalf.
- The vehicle you will use to reach it.
- The general messages.
- The timeline/deadline.

- The tasks associated with the project.
- The point person for the overall project, and the designated individuals assigned each task.

This plan should reflect your business and target specific stakeholders.

Does your newsletter need to reach your donors and inspire them to give, give more, or give again? Then it shouldn't also go to your food bank clients living at the poverty level. Is your brochure meant to spell out the importance of mitigating climate change? Then it shouldn't include a tutorial on the importance of endowments.

Every time ask yourself these questions: Who are you trying to reach and how can you do that most effectively, with which vehicle and with what messaging? And how does each effort feed into your fundraising and programmatic goals?

A marketing plan will outline all of this. And just as important, it will tell you which efforts really *aren't* doing anything toward your goal. A blog that doesn't get people to act on your behalf is just a self-serving way to talk about yourself. A blog that inspires a certain crowd of people to talk to each other about the importance of your organization and gets them to attend your next fundraiser has a purpose.

As you create your marketing strategies, there are a few phenomena to consider. These will help drive your strategies and determine how successful they are. Or not.

They also illustrate my love for metaphors.

I present to you the Needle versus Haystack Theory and the Weed and Seed Effect.

The Needle Versus Haystack Theory

As organizations set about creating their marketing strategies, they must first determine whether they are what I call a haystack organization or a needle organization.

Haystack organizations have missions with broad appeal. They are organizations that focus on an issue that affects many, many people, an issue that has momentum in the media, a mission that, as people hear about it, will spark more than just a moment of interest around your cause. Instead, many members of this broad audience will find the mission relevant enough—to themselves, their lives, or the lives of people they know—that they will be inspired to act when they hear about it, and help the organization reach its goals as a result.

A needle organization has a mission that's just as important to those it serves, but is less relevant to a broad audience. It brings with it important stories, but fewer of them, and statistics that also tend to be smaller in number. The work of the organization is more specific: helping people live with a unique disease, creating theater for a specific community, or raising money for a particular school district. Needle organizations do important work, but they don't impact most people and therefore their missions aren't as relatable to a broader audience. Will they care about your cause when they hear about it? Probably. Will they take action or give to it afterward? Not likely.

This can be a harsh reality for needle organizations, who feel so passionate about their missions. But it's important that they understand this reality if they're going to truly reach their goals.

I created the Needle Versus Haystack metaphor when I first launched my company to help clarify why some organizations were meeting their marketing goals while others failed. I had two clients who illustrated this metaphor perfectly. The first focused on environmental issues, specifically geared toward keeping the community beautiful through air pollution reduction. The second was an organization focusing on people living with a very specific brain abnormality, which affected their motor function.

The environmental organization was classic haystack. People—especially those in Southern California where I lived—*love* their environment. They know full well that they are lucky, lucky individuals. And one of the reasons they have such a great quality of life is the outdoors—the weather, the cleanliness, the opportunities to engage in all kinds of sports.

This organization had the opportunity to bring in new stakeholders more easily than many others. Why? Because its work, its stories, and its statistics resonated with just about everybody in town.

The organization that provided services for the brain abnormality was needle through and through. This organization does incredible work. The stories are inspiring, and, for those it helps, play a critical role in people's lives. Yet most people, while caring about the organization in the moment they hear about it, can't truly relate to the mission. When I worked with this organization there were about 1,000 people living with this disease in all of San Diego County (population exceeding 3 million), with an additional 15 new cases each year. And so getting the broader public to act or give on behalf of the organization (instead, remember, of acting on behalf of another) was a significantly tougher task. Reaching out to the whole haystack (through vehicles like the media) and hoping to find new supporters who were interested enough to act and give on its behalf was an inefficient strategy at best, a waste of time at worst.

My recommendations?

I told the environmental organization to get out there. Reach out through the media and let people know about the work they do to make the community even better for future generations. Reach out to new people through events and newspaper stories. Be the leader in keeping the region beautiful and clean, and you will be a hero.

I told the other organization to find those needles first, then hit them hard. Expensive media campaigns would not be worth it, because hitting that whole haystack with their stories, while compelling, would not make them relevant to most people. It certainly wouldn't make it relevant enough to get them to give.

Instead, we identified those groups most likely to resonate with their stories. We talked about the people the organization served and their circles of families, friends, and supporters. Would they give? Were there partner organizations that would provide access to new stakeholders? What about volunteers who had connections to the cause, who cared about it deeply? What about medical facilities? Once we figured out who these needles were, the organization reached out to them directly with beautiful materials and meaningful e-blasts. This more targeted strategy was not just better, but smarter. The organization saved the money they would have otherwise spent on media campaigns, and focused their energy and resources on those more likely to give, act, and tell the organizational story to others.

A WORD OF WARNING...

As you reflect on the Needles Versus Haystack concept, chances are you, your staff, your board, and others will first decide you are a haystack organization. After all, if you all care about your cause so deeply, doesn't it stand to figure that others do as well?

Not necessarily.

Do your best to take a step back, imagine you are a member of the general public, and determine whether you could truly relate to the cause. Talk about it with your staff and your board. Talk about it with external people who have no stake and ask them to be honest.

- If they heard your story on the news, would they care? They will say yes.
- Would they give? They will say yes.
- Would they really? Ask them to be honest.
- Would their colleagues at work give? Would their families? Their friends? Really?

Ask them to be brutally honest. That's when you'll have your answer.

The Weed and Seed Effect

Joe, one of my best buddies in college, spent a summer working at a store that specialized in landscaping products. He came back with a tale that I thought so brilliant, I now use it to illustrate something all of us in the marketing world have been guilty of at one time or another. I call it the Weed and Seed Effect.

One day a customer approached Joe with a product called Weed and Seed, and asked if it worked. Joe wasn't sure, but his boss piped in and replied, "Well, it weeds…and it seeds…but it doesn't do either *particularly well*."

How often do we try to find efficient solutions to our problems that actually do a few things, but halfway? A newsletter that targets both our clients and our donors, a brochure that explains our annual giving program and the upcoming shows at our theater. If your organization is using marketing to create materials that appeal to different audiences for different purposes, you just might be weeding and seeding.

Incidentally, this effect can also be seen at the gym (what if I squeeze my butt *while* I'm running on the treadmill?), at the liquor store (ever heard of blush?), and when we hold staff meetings to explain a restructure and then celebrate someone's birthday.

Pick one thing and do it well. Don't cut corners if it means you do two or more things poorly. If you cannot afford two brochures, you might need to make some hard choices. You need to figure out which goals are most important, who will help you achieve them, and how to best reach them using which messages. This is a tall order for one marketing project. If you try meeting two goals with one piece, you are setting yourself up for failure.

Chapter 38

THE MOST COMMON MARKETING MISTAKE WE MAKE—AND HOW TO AVOID IT

There are plenty of marketing pitfalls many of us fall into. I've already talked about a few.

But here's the granddaddy of them all...the biggest mistake people make when it comes to marketing their organizations.

This one is bigger than not having a goal or not having a plan. This one is bigger than a Weed and Seed brochure or putting your issue out on the broadcast news when you really appeal to only a dozen people.

Ready?

The biggest marketing mistake people make is failing to think like the consumer.

You know your organization is important. You believe in it down to the very core of who you are. You just know that if you explain everything, tell a dozen stories, and give all the details about why you matter, that people will get it and give to it.

Wrong.

I ask you this: How many paragraphs of long text does it take to get your eyes to glaze over when reading a brochure? Or an ad? Or a newspaper article? How do you feel when you open up a newsletter and see thick, chunky paragraphs squeezed in upon themselves in teeny type and no margins, just because the organization *had* to make all of these very important points—the points that would collectively get you to understand its plight, see the light, and give, give, give? Do you ever get to the end?

Yes, your organization is important. But you should not explain every single little detail as to why. How many people want to be inundated with that kind of message? How many will actually read it all? How many people will get through the first paragraph?

Zero.

If you want your marketing to be effective, if you want people to experience it and act in a way that reaches your organizational goals, you must reduce any barriers to their getting your message. You must think like the consumer.

What does this mean?

- Boil it down into creative, succinct, inspirational language.
- Talk in quick quips.
- Give the equivalent of written sound bites.
- Don't have a mission *paragraph*, have a mission *statement.*
- Give up the biggest goods first on what you do and why you matter, then boil them down to a few, focused comments.
- Include lots of graphics.
- And for goodness sake, let there be white space!

I worked for an organization in New York where the CEO directed me to create an annual report 100 pages long.

100 pages.

Know how many people read it all?

Two. Me, because I had to write it. And my CEO.

Know this: If you write too much, explain too much, or talk too much, people will stop reading or listening. They will stop paying attention. More is not better.

A Few Words on Writing

This brings me to my next point, and that's about writing in general.

I give it its own section because writing is so important, not just to marketing, but to *everything.*

If you are in any way managing or leading an organization—as the ED, the marketer, the development director, or a board member—and you can't write well, you need to learn. Simple as that.

Yes, some of this skill comes naturally and we can't all be organically stellar at it. But that's no excuse not to do your best in this arena. Writing, especially technical writing, can be learned. It can be practiced until you are able to get your point across articulately and in a way that reflects the professionalism and credibility of your organization.

As a leader or manager, your effectiveness relies in large part on how you communicate what you do—and how you get others to understand and act as a result.

Every email you send, every speech you give, every article you write in every newsletter must be thought through. Do not think that a rushed piece of sloppy writing is going to get you anything positive. It will get you noticed, but for all the wrong reasons.

Can you write well? Great! Practice and get even better at it.

Need to learn to write better? Read a book or take a class. Notice how other leaders you respect—in the nonprofit and other sectors—communicate. Then try to emulate their tone and style.

And practice. Do it over and over. Check your emails before they go out and give your direct mail solicitations a good, thorough review before sending them on. Have others read your communication before you release it. Always consider what you would think about a certain piece of writing if you received it—and what you would think about the person behind it.

Your writing must be technically pristine as well as persuasive. These are not mutually exclusive. After all, just because a book is nonfiction doesn't mean it's not a compelling read. (Just look at the one you've got in your hand right now!)

Your writing must be excellent. Accurate. Grammatically correct. You must be succinct. You must be compelling. You must sell.

ARE YOU WRITING TOO MUCH?

First of all, you probably are. I'm a pretty succinct writer, yet I find I can cut almost everything I write by at least a third once I take a break and read it over. It hurts, yes, because it's easy to fall in love with our own writing. Nevertheless, in the end, I want people to read it.

Here's a good test. If you're writing a direct mail piece or a flyer and you find yourself playing with the margins to fit it all on one page, stop. Cut it. I promise you can. And the final product will be much better.

Chapter 39

THE LUXURY OF A MARKETING PROFESSIONAL AND WHAT TO DO IF YOU DON'T HAVE ONE

If you have a marketing specialist on staff, congratulations! Support this person, help him or her develop professionally, and make sure your specialist know the latest trends in the craft.

If you don't, do not think you can simply put a fundraiser or another staff member in the role and create a great marketing strategy. (Poor, poor events people. They always seem to get this extra special role.) You must either find those who already know the ins and outs of marketing or you must train them.

What do you do if you don't have someone on staff to fill this role, but you truly believe (as I hope you by now do) marketing is a worthwhile endeavor for your organization?

A few ideas:

- Ask around at other nonprofits and find out who in your community understands marketing and has proven success in it. If you can find someone who specifically understands the nonprofit sector and how to succeed in getting various markets to act in a way that achieves its organizational goals, all the better.
- Begin to form relationships with these people. Try to find those who have some kind of connection to your cause. Woo them. Charm them.
- Get them involved. One great way to do this is to create a marketing committee and have them head it up. Consider who else might sit on the committee, such as fundraising

staff/volunteers, key program staff, board members, and others who can contribute the information needed to build your message and your plan. (For more on building effective committees, see page 105.)

- If the marketing expert you find turns out to be both effective and invested in your cause, consider bringing this person onto your board. (*However*, don't do this until you are sure the person both knows his/her marketing stuff and is the right fit for your board; see page 52.)

- If you cannot find someone to volunteer in this capacity, then you may need to pony up. You will still need to identify great marketers who—and this is important—have nonprofit experience. Then find out what it will cost to have them create a marketing plan and potentially help you execute it. It might not be as much as you think, and it might be worth it to move some funds around to make it happen.

If you can help it, don't get all of your marketing done by begging a firm to do it pro bono. This is a terrible way to begin a relationship with a consultant. (See page 112.) The relationship needs to be equal and professional, and you need to feel okay providing critical feedback. If you look for free first, you might sacrifice skill. And even if you get the best marketing person possible, if you don't pay this person you will fall to the bottom of the queue regularly. There's just no other option for many people. They've got bills to pay, too.

MEASURING YOUR MARKETING EFFORTS

Measuring the impact of your marketing efforts is a tricky thing. Marketing is more subjective than fundraising, where the ultimate measure is often the dollar deposited into your bank. Because it's more elusive, we tend to avoid trying to measure our marketing in a way that's truly meaningful. And, let's be honest, we're a bit nervous about what it means if we start doing so and find out our marketing isn't working all that well. And so we avoid it all the more.

But...

If we really want to do good *well*, we know we can't.

Where do we begin? By asking the market itself.

Include questions at every turn that ask how someone found out about you. Hold a focus group with your stakeholders and ask them what works and what doesn't in your materials. If an event hits budget, ask participants whether the marketing helped. If it doesn't hit budget, ask anyway.

Build in one or more of the many online and easier-than-ever analytical tools to help you figure out which messages are driving people to your website, and what they click on when they get there. And of course, set goals before you do any of this so you have something to measure against.

As always, research what works best right now and ask similar organizations how they do it.

One other point on this...

Want to know if your new materials, updated website, or direct mail will be effective *before* you implement them? Ask your markets.

Pull together people you trust who represent your donors, clients, members, or other audiences you will target with your materials, and ask them what works and what doesn't. Then take it all with a grain of salt and adjust accordingly. Your odds of success might go way up.

Chapter 40

PUBLIC RELATIONS/MEDIA

Media is just one piece of the overall marketing strategy, but it's a biggie. And while public relations follows many of the marketing principles already discussed, it's also its own animal in many ways. It's got its own culture and its own parameters, and it can be tricky to use it the right way—the way that meets your organizational goals.

Let's begin with a fact.

Organizations love to write press releases. I've seen it suggested by boards and staff members everywhere. And I get it. It seems like an obvious strategy—get the media to pay attention to your organization and they will get it to lots of people, who will then be inspired by your message and care enough to respond to it.

A nice idea, but a total myth. Let's explore why.

The Point of PR

Getting your organization's name in the paper makes you feel good. But is that enough? Is that alone worth your organization's time and resources? What role is PR really supposed to play?

It's a familiar tune.

The role of public relations is to inspire people to act on behalf of your organization to help reach its goals.

Remember the Needle Versus Haystack Theory? (See page 215.) Before creating a media strategy, you must make sure that reaching out to the whole haystack makes sense—that it will help you achieve your organizational goals.

If you actually get a story, what are the odds enough of those people will act in the way you want them to in order to reach your goal? Are these odds good enough, and will the outcome be good enough, that it's worth putting your time and energy into a media plan/pitch in the first place?

Ask the questions and be realistic with the answers. And know that sometimes the glory and fame of a story in the paper won't get you much—except a cool clipping to send your family.

Now, there will be times when PR does make sense, even if it won't reach your biggest organizational goals.

- Sometimes you'll want to get a new board member announced in the paper because you know it will make that person feel good, which can only help your relationship.
- Sometimes you'll announce that a new corporate partner has come on board because you want that company to know how much you appreciate it.
- Sometimes your CEO will be listed in the "Top CEOs of the City" story because you want others to know you've got a great leader.

These goals aren't wrong. Just be honest about them, and know up front that you're spending organizational resources to get them done. And understand what might not get done as a result.

What the Media Is Good For

As you set about your media strategy and determine whether or not it makes sense for your organization to engage in one, it's helpful to keep in mind just what the media *is* good for.

I present some of these things now:

Stories about your organization that will get people to act on its behalf
Sometimes you have a great story—a success story related to your mission that is relatable to a lot of people, a story that is timely because

you're the cancer society and it's National Cancer Awareness month. In these cases you *should* pitch the media because chances are they will cover you—and because you have fully thought through what you want the audience to do and explicitly stated it.

Promotion of events
Chances are there are calendar listings all over your town, which people look to when making their recreational plans. Make sure your events are in there.

Op-eds/Letters to the editor to show expertise
You need to not just show that you do good work, but to show you do it *well*, that you're the best at it. Proving your expertise will lend you credibility, which will make you stand out from your competition. Opinion/editorial articles and letters show that you know what you're talking about, that you've got a knowledge base that is strong and up-to-date, and that you want to share it to advance your community in some way. If you make yourself the go-to resource on an issue, individuals will think of you first when they want to get involved or contribute to a cause.

Sponsorships
Media sponsorships aren't what they used to be. When I worked for a broadcast affiliate, we would partner with nonprofit organizations to promote their events through public service announcements during pretty decent time slots. This is not the case anymore.

Nowadays the media is struggling to figure out its own relevancy. Many media outlets are losing dollars at an alarming rate. As a result, they choose their partnerships even more carefully, and often won't partner with you unless you bring in a third party, usually a for-profit corporation, to underwrite your ad time (known as the Corporate Social Responsibility model).

Just as with all fundraising initiatives around corporations, your job is to convince the media prospect of what they'll get out of the bargain if they partner with you (see page 177). They must full understand how having their logo on your materials and their presence at your event will bring them new audience members and generate ratings—and therefore dollars—for their companies.

One important thing to know: Media sponsorships rarely come with cash. In fact, I've never seen it happen. The media's end of the bargain is usually production and ad space. Sometimes they'll get one of their personalities to emcee your event. They usually don't promise editorial stories, though they often come through on this in the end.

Advertising

I'm actually not a big proponent of spending hard-earned nonprofit dollars on advertising, but it bears mentioning here because it *is* one way for organizations to get promotion. They just need to pay for it. With the exception of a carefully placed announcement of an incredibly relevant event, I haven't found advertising to be effective—certainly not effective enough to warrant the thousands of dollars some organizations pour into it.

If your organization has the luxury of an advertising budget, think it through. Who are you trying to reach, and how do you know they will pay attention to an ad? Where will you place it? How big will it be? And what do you want consumers to do once they've experienced it?

Make sure you have good odds of meeting your organizational goals through advertising before making this investment. Otherwise, you're throwing your money away.

Chapter 41

THE PRESS RELEASE

So, you've thought it through, decided the haystack is your audience, and figured out what you want them to do once they experience your story in the media. You've also determined what the media will be good for in your case, and how you can use them to meet your organizational goals.

Now how do you get your story in there?

You begin by writing a great press release.

Though the latest trends in technology and social media have some believing otherwise, I still believe in the press release as one of your first tactics to create media interest. It encapsulates your story and, if done correctly, gets it very succinctly and strategically into the hands of those who make coverage decisions.

A few tips on writing an effective release:

- Keep it brief. You don't need a ton of copy, and the media won't read it all anyway. Include the journalistic basics (who, what, where, when, why, and how) and perhaps a compelling quote from someone who can add a bit of flavor to the event or topic and why it's important.
- Start with a great headline—just like they'll have to do when they report on it.
- Give the logistical and contact details up front, and then repeat them at the end.
- Explicitly state why this is a story that will matter to their audience, what kinds of interviews you can provide, and ideas for visuals (video for broadcast, photos for print).
- Make it convenient. When you are explicitly clear, when

you spoon-feed the media the relevancy, the details, the interviews, and the visuals, it's very tempting for them to move ahead with your story. These are busy people working in a chaotic business. You need to remove any possible barrier to their coverage of your story. You need to commit to getting them what they need when they need it. If you're not willing to do this, then don't pitch it at all.

- Know that you really have a story. If you are going to convince the media that your story is truly relevant, you must first know what a relevant story *is*. It sounds simple, but when I was an assignment editor I threw away about 85 percent of the press releases I received. Why? Because they weren't stories. Nonprofits thought I'd care about their golf tournament when it had virtually no real impact for my very broad, very haystack audience. A true media story is relevant to most people. It is also timely, and usually episodic—relating to a specific occasion or event, as opposed to an ongoing campaign or program of some kind. Make sure you're pitching a story. Trust me, the media will not forget those who do...or those who don't.

- A final word on press releases: Make sure you include your contact name, and the best way to reach you at any time of day or night. The media works on a 24-hour cycle, and if you want to play with them you need to do so as well. Not having your cell phone number on there presents a barrier. Chances are they won't have the time or interest to overcome it.

The Follow-up

Once you've sent the press release, you can't stop there. All kinds of things can happen to the release, and it's the follow-up pitch—usually over the phone—that will often get you the story you're looking for.

The Pitch

Some tips on the pitch:

- Know *when* to pitch. Do not call a broadcast news station at 5:05 p.m. That's when their newscast is going on and they are most likely setting up live shots, coordinating breaking news, and dealing with reporters out in the field. Call early in the morning or mid-afternoon, when they might have a moment to talk. Wait until the day before or the morning of a news event before you call to follow up. The media is worried about the news of the day, not the news of next week (though do make sure you send the press release at least a week early to get it in their files).

- Know *how* to pitch. When you get them on the phone, don't keep them long. Don't talk all about the background of your story. Thank them for a few seconds of their time, and then tell them you just want to make sure they got your release about story XXX, which is important because of XXX, for which they can put together a great story because they can talk to XXX and use XXX as visuals. Then ask them if they need anything else.

- Know *where* to pitch. If you want to get your upcoming event in a community calendar, don't call the main news desk. If you want to get your arts event covered, don't call the education reporter. If you want to reach a specific community about something relevant to them, don't use your city's main newspaper, which won't care. Don't waste anybody's time because you didn't do your homework.

- Know *who* to pitch. Just as with most everything else, success in public relations is all about who you know. Form relationships with members of the media and find those who care most about your cause. Don't bug them too much but follow up with them, target them with your pitches in a way that will resonate with them, become

their go-to *resource* on issues related to your cause, and
build trust and friendship. It's a whole lot more effective to
call Steve, the education reporter who likes you and knows
you'll come through on your story about your scholarship
program, than to cold call the assignment desk.

- Get creative. Make your press release stand out. Send along
  treats or food, something related to the event that will
  intrigue the person who gets it. Just don't get too hokey.

- Make it timely. There is a reason this is called the "news."
  The media are thinking about the stories they need to
  cover and the news holes they need to fill *today*. Don't give
  them a story that isn't immediately relevant. Big, fun,
  colorful festivals might get coverage. A capital campaign
  won't, unless there's a major launch event before it starts or
  a glitzy ribbon-cutting after it's over.

- Be the expert. Become *the* source for your cause, the one
  the media will call if they have a story that relates to your
  mission in any way. Demonstrate that *you* know your
  stuff and, even more important, that you know how to be
  responsive to *their* needs. Remember, make it convenient
  and they will return again and again.

Chapter 42

THE INTERVIEW

So you've pitched the media and gotten an interview. Congratulations! Now don't blow it.

There are a number of ways to make an interview successful, and they are somewhat nuanced based on whether you are going broadcast (and are being recorded using a camera or tape recorder) or print (and someone else is writing down what you say).

The Broadcast Interview

In a lot of ways, broadcast (TV/radio) is better than print because you are on tape, stating what you need to state, and it doesn't need to be translated through a reporter who writes it down, then publishes it. At the same time, that means your message is all *you*, so know how to get the most out of it.

The number-one way to do this is to keep control of your message.

Here are a few tips:

Tip 1: Speak in sound bites…or they'll decide what you say.
Learn how to encapsulate your message into 10 to 15 seconds. That's about how long reporters/editors will let your sound bite go on before they hear channels turning all over town. If you go on and on about why your cause is important, the editor will cut your message for you, which means you've lost control of the message.

Tip 2: Don't be afraid to start a sound bite over.
It can be nerve-wracking to sit in front of a camera and talk about your organization. If this is a taped interview and you find yourself stumbling or not getting to your point succinctly, look at the reporter and say that you're going to start over. The camera will keep rolling, so just pause for a second, take a breath, and begin again. Better that than for you to spend your golden media opportunity stumbling inarticulately on camera.

Tip 3: Know how to handle a live interview.
Being live—sitting on a news set or on location from your event site, for instance—can produce an even greater level of anxiety, so prepare yourself. Ask the interviewer ahead of time what will be asked, talk slowly, and have your points down. Have those points written, in large type, in front of you so that you can refer to specific statistics or other information during the interview. Once the cameras are rolling, speak to the reporter as though he or she is a donor sitting across the table from you, and not to the thousands of people watching you at that very moment. Otherwise the whole idea can get overwhelming and take you off your game.

Print Interviews

Print interviews can be disconcerting as well. They often happen over the phone, so you hear the reporter's fingers tapping away on the keyboard as you speak, and as you hope that he or she is getting your message down correctly. Even when these interviews happen in person, you don't know what the reporter is writing down as you speak. You don't know that your listener *gets it.*

A few tips to make sure they do:

Tip 1: Learn to speak slowly and intentionally.
No explanation needed, right?

Tip 2: Go off the record if you mess up.

If you feel you've said something that, seconds after it's out of your mouth, feels less than appropriate, tell the reporter it was off the record. Reporters don't have to honor this, but if they have integrity they will feel as though they do. If they don't, then brace yourself and hope for the best. And by the way, do your best to make this a nonissue by avoiding the mistake in the first place.

Tip 3: Prepare to see the finished product when everybody else does— not before.

Don't bother asking if you can get a preview of a story before it is released. They simply don't provide that.

COMMON MEDIA MISTAKES

During both my time in the media business and my time in the nonprofit sector, I've seen a set of common mistakes. I've addressed them somewhat in this section, but allow me to compile my favorite list for easy access.

Do not:

- Make the media work too hard for your story. If they need to read too much, if you don't help them meet their deadlines, if you don't get them the information, interviews, or visuals you promised, then don't bother calling them again.
- Call them at 5:05 p.m. Show them you know when they are busy—and when they are most likely screwing around in their cubes—by calling mid-morning or early afternoon.
- Make the pitch too long. They simply don't care enough.
- Assume they care about your cause as much as you do. They don't.
- Get them to cover an event that looks like it could turn out to be a bust. If you have to gather a cluster of people together and ask the camera to point at them so it looks like more

people attended than really did, the media will not return. Make sure your story is feasible, your interview articulate, and your event a probable success before getting the media to cover it.

- Fail to ask the audience to do what you want them to do in order to achieve your goals. If you get an interview, don't forget you're doing this for a specific purpose. Clearly tell the audience what you need, and ask the reporter to make sure they include it.
- Fail to tell the audience how to do what you need them to do. If you ask people to donate to your cause but don't give them your website or phone number, shame on you.

Chapter 43

THERE IS NO BAD PR: THE GREAT FALLACY

Sometimes you don't need to go to the media, because they'll come to you.

And sometimes this is a good thing. If there's breaking news about your cause and they want some good information and perspective, choosing you to provide it lends tremendous credibility.

But ...

Sometimes, when the media comes knocking, it's not a good thing. At all.

Perhaps a fired staff member has told all kinds of bad stories about your organization, or your big event used a whole lot more money to produce than it made and this information has gotten out (donors don't like that). Maybe the salary of one of your staff members is unusually high and someone took a good look at your organization's tax return.

When you face a PR crisis, you need to handle it with absolute, pristine care. Be clear that being in the media spotlight is not necessarily a good thing for you. Better to never be featured on the airwaves again than to have something negative said about you. Audience perception is reality, and if you think nonprofits are off-limits you're dead wrong. In fact, some reporters make it their business to expose stories about nonprofits and how they might be squandering taxpayer dollars or executing their programs unethically.

Facing a PR Crisis?

First, breathe deeply. You'll get through this.

Then…

Get in front of it.

If a story comes out about your organization, work with whoever is most appropriate on your staff and board to develop a succinct, clear response. Then, put it out to everyone you know, including the media itself. Make sure your donors, volunteers, board members, and staff all know the message, in the event they are asked about it. Be transparent and sincere. Write a response and submit it as a letter to the editor. Ask community members and other stakeholders— specifically those not paid by the organization—to do the same.

Use those contacts.

Now is the time to cash in on those media relationships you worked so hard to cultivate. Call your greatest media champions and try to get some face time. I was hit hard with a media crisis once and called my favorite reporter, who worked for a lead media station in town. When I explained the situation, her words came easily.

"Deirdre," she said, "meet me at 2 p.m. and I will give you as much time on camera as you need to get your side of the story out."

Do not think it will go away.

I was conducting a session on PR to a group of nonprofits leaders, and one of them asked me how to shake the media off when they get a bite on a story and won't leave you alone. A reporter had apparently been calling her repeatedly because he'd gotten a juicy tidbit, and she found herself ignoring the calls and hoping he'd go away.

My answer? He won't.

When reporters get something on your organization—true or not—and believe it to be a real story that will get the public's attention, there is no such thing as shaking them off.

You must address the issue. If you don't, it will get out there anyway, and you'll lose all control of your message.

Try not to do anything illegal or unethical.
Of course, the easiest way to be transparent and sincere, and to have your messages be effective during a PR crisis, is to have truth and integrity on your side. If you screwed up accidentally, consider owning that from the beginning. If you or one of your stakeholders did something untoward and knew about it—perhaps you should be squirming a bit anyway.

Chapter 44

THE ROLE OF SOCIAL MEDIA

These days many people believe social media is *the thing*.
- It's the thing that will get your organization noticed.
- It's the thing that will get your organization to prove it is cutting-edge.
- It's the thing that will help your organization reach its fundraising goals.

It probably won't surprise you to hear me say I have a different take on social media.

Social media in itself is a tool, one that needs to be used specifically and strategically to...wait for it...meet your organizational goals.

As with many of the other marketing tools I've discussed, social media is just one vehicle to get your message out there. If you use it, you need to determine that this is where a specific segment of your markets hangs out—a segment that will act in a way that will help you get things done and reach your goals. And that you know how to find that segment, *and* that you can create messages that will get you what you need.

Far too often these days, nonprofits embrace social media because they feel as though they *should*. They feel this way for lots of reasons:
- They hear how it helped other organizations meet fundraising goals.
- Their boards want them to show that they are up-and-coming.
- They somehow truly believe that people will click on the

link of a social media post that highlights your staff member of the month. (They won't. Would you?)

It seems as if every day one of my clients is telling me how he or she launched a new social media page, and every day my first question is…why?

Like all things marketing, like all things in your *organization*, social media takes time to do well, and so should be done only if it's worth it, which means it will help you reach your goals. If you choose to go this route, know where your markets hang out within the social media realm, and identify how best to get them engaged through these channels.

Do not kid yourself that simply reminding people that you exist through an update every so often will help you make budget. It won't happen.

'Nuff said.

Doing Marketing Well

Marketing is one of the messiest parts of running the nonprofit business. It's somewhat subjective. It involves artistic expression. It's hard to define, and even harder to measure.

Yet, if taken seriously, if executed as part of a larger strategy that targets specific people and asks them to do specific things, it can take your organization to a whole new level—a new level of giving, a new level of credibility, and a new level of professionalism.

In the end, good marketing isn't just good business.

It makes your organization a better one.

PART FIVE

MEASUREMENT

Chapter 45

WHAT MEASUREMENT REALLY IS

I know. Of all of the Ms, this one is the least sexy, the least passion-filled, the least nonprofit. It's the one that makes eyes glaze over. It's the one that is perhaps hardest to understand, and even harder to create.

What Most People Think

In our minds, measurement is:

- Tedious, impersonal, and not at all connected to the passion of our mission.
- Not as important as getting the programs done.
- Something only specially trained people can do.

The Truth

Measurement is just as critical as—and in some cases more than—the other three Ms.

The truth is, measurement:

- Proves your worth to every single stakeholder.
- Shows that you are meeting your goals.
- Allows you to make good decisions.
- Illustrates your commitment to excellence, strategy, and integrity.
- Makes you stand out from your competition.
- Can be done in-house if needed, and within a fairly quick time frame.

The Good News

It is possible to do measurement well.

First of all—trust me when I say this—you know more about this than you think you do. You know your organization and what it's supposed to be doing. You know your programs. You know your clients. You have a sense of what's working and what isn't. You understand your current level of general client satisfaction and the reasons behind it.

Your next step—achieved through measurement—is to quantify it, to either validate what you already know or bring about a new understanding. This is not about embracing scientific terms like statistical validation. It's not about reams of spreadsheets. It's about putting a concrete value to your organization and its impact. It's about understanding what you're truly doing for people—understanding if and how you're really meeting your mission.

- It doesn't just tell you that your organization is reducing the number of smokers, but how many, and for how long.
- It doesn't just show that people are engaging in and enjoying your theater productions, but just how many are coming—and how many are coming back.
- It doesn't just tell you the number of people sleeping in your shelter, but the number of people who are using that time to get stabilized and develop their skills, then find work.

Once you know how you're doing—concretely—then you can act on it, grow it, and learn from it. Measurement makes you better, and, when done correctly, lets everyone else know it.

And the best part is, few organizations *do* do it well, which makes you stand out all the more if you do.

TO BE CLEAR...

This section focuses on the outcome measurement of your *programs*.

There are other initiatives that will help you measure other components of your organization, such as your corporate partnerships or the ROI on your events. Those are covered back in the money section. (See page 163.)

You will also want to measure the impact of your marketing efforts, which we covered in the marketing section. (See page 225.)

This M is about the true impact of your services and how they achieve your mission.

Behavior change, self-sufficiency, and satisfaction on the part of those you serve are all involved. It can get messy, yes, but that doesn't mean you can't do it.

So please don't skip this section. While there may be reasons to bring in outside help for some pieces, *you* can lead the way to an effective outcome measurement program for your organization.

I promise.

Chapter 46

WHY MEASUREMENT IS MORE IMPORTANT THAN EVER

Measuring your work is *always* important.

It's the only way to truly know how you're doing, first as an organization and then as compared to similar organizations.

In fact, if you don't engage in measurement, those first three *M*s don't mean a whole lot. But many of us hate it anyway.

Often, and I myself have done this plenty, we tend to think of measurement as a complete and total headache. It takes time to set up our outcome measures and our indicators, it takes time to figure out just who is going to collect and enter them, and it takes time to figure out what to do with them once we've got them.

On top of that, outcomes do more than highlight where you're organization is excelling. They also show where it isn't—and then you have to fix it.

Four Reasons Measurement Is Important

These are all reasons why you might not want to engage in measurement. But here's why you have to:

Reason 1. Your organization needs to know.
Outcome measures tell you how you're doing, what you're doing great, and what you need to work on. It's your job to know this stuff and act on it. Period.

Reason 2. Funders are curious.

More and more these days, government and private funders are interested in your outcomes, and might be the ones that push you to begin your outcome measurement program. Just like the rest of us, they've got to explain to their boards and their community members why they made certain choices about whom to fund. And they have to show the money is being used well.

Reason 3. Donors are getting savvy.

A few factors have come together and caused individual donors to get savvier about measures. They've heard about scandals where donations given to an organization haven't been used well or in the way it was promised they would be. And so they want to know more, specifically about how their dollars are being used for true impact.

It's also getting easier for donors to get your information. Where at one time few people knew just what the heck a Form 990 was, now there are all kinds of new technological and digital tools that provide access to information about your organization with very little effort. And donors are using them.

A WORD OF CAUTION ON DONORS

There is one downside to providing your measures to others. I've seen instances where donors get outcome information on your organization, don't completely agree with what you're doing, and start to make requests or even demands about how you need to do things differently. I encourage you to work with them in a reasonable way, but do not allow yourself to create all kinds of programmatic changes to please a donor. There are too many of them, each with his or her own passion and opinion. You know your organization best. You understand what your mission strives to do and how your strategies will achieve it. Donors might be helping to pay for things, but that doesn't give them license to determine how your programs work. If a donor thinks you need to target seniors as part of your smoking cessation program but your organization has decided to focus on youth, then you need to help that donor understand the reasons why. A donor who can't might need to find another organization that better fits his or her priorities.

Reason 4. Your competition is doing it.

If you haven't figured this out by now, this M is not my favorite. Unlike marketing or management, it's a bit too impersonal, a bit technical for my taste.

But...

I do believe in it, I do know how important it is, and I do know that organizations that want to set themselves up for success need to be in this game.

Your competition is.

Other nonprofits are in this same measurement boat, working with funders and donors and boards to figure out how to measure their impact. They are creating reports and working through tedious data collection projects. And in the end, they're doing it for the same reasons you are.

This means that if your measurement system is not strategic and strong, you are at a direct disadvantage against your competition. Even if you're doing great work and they are only performing at a standard level, they can show what they are achieving and you cannot.

Chapter 47

MEASUREMENT—GETTING STARTED

As with every other M, the most important thing is to know what you want to achieve through your outcome measurement program before you begin—what you want to know (and tell others) at the end that you didn't know at the start.

Once you know what you want to learn, create a strategy that will get you that information. Get specific and make the information you collect meaningful. Think through the following questions:

- What kind of information will tell you what you want to know?
- What kind of data will you need to collect and how will you do so?
- Should you use surveys or focus groups to get a sense of the effectiveness of your programs?
- How will you input your data? Into what system? Who will do so and how often?
- What kind of technology will help you track and communicate with your stakeholders effectively?
- Who will help get the data out, review it, and analyze it?

Make the most of your outcome measurement program right from the start. Talk to donors and funders, and ask them what they want to see. Talk to other organizations about how they track meaningful outcomes.

Try to think differently. Embrace outcome measurement. Know it will make your organization better. Know it will make you stand way, way out. Know it won't be as tedious or as painful as you think it will. And spread this new message to your staff.

After all, you're all in this one together.

Now, let's get started.

MEASUREMENT LINGO

Before getting started, let's work through the measurement lingo. This is the kind of thing that can trip people up. Allow me to clarify the pieces to this puzzle.

Inputs

Inputs are the components from within your organization that will be used in the program's activities and processes. They include staff, equipment, money, et cetera.

They are the costs of the work to get the program done.

If we're looking at a smoking cessation workshop series, examples of inputs are the staff and volunteers running the sessions, the IT equipment needed to facilitate the conversation and then record or input it, and the space for the sessions.

Activities

Activities are the processes in the program that get the work done. They use active words such as *feeding, clothing, teaching,* and *counseling.*

In our smoking cessation example, they are the sessions themselves and the teaching/dialogue that occurs as part of the process.

Outputs

Outputs are the beans in the term *bean counting*: the quantity of the activities completed. They are the units related to your program. They include things like the number of people served, the amount of food distributed, or the number of theater productions you put on in a given year. In our smoking cessation program, they would include the number of sessions and the number of participants per session.

Some people love outputs—they think they tell a whole lot about the program. In fact, some organizations get the outputs and stop right there. Sometimes funders encourage it.

The truth, however, is that alone, outputs do not tell you much—if anything—about the actual impact of your program. Ultimately it's not about the number of people sheltered today, but instead the number of people who become stabilized enough at the shelter to find permanent housing in the future, return to work, and get healthier.

Even if you're tempted to talk up outputs instead of outcomes, which happens because outputs are easier to count and easier to wrap your head around, I challenge you to take it to the next level. Be more intentional and meaningful in defining your impact, and your stakeholders will be impressed. And they should be.

Outcomes

Outcomes are the impact of your program.

They reflect the true benefits of the inputs/activities and outputs. They tell you whether or not your program is effectively meeting your mission and your goals.

Outcomes are often communicated in terms of knowledge, skills, and behaviors.

Think about the number of people you want to impact and *how you will know you've done so*. Think harder than most and you'll be more effective than most.

- How many people do you want to come to three of your theater productions because they came to the first and liked it enough to come to two more?
- What percentage of your participants do you want to reflect back to you a new kind of understanding about an environmental issue? To begin recycling their cans now that they have a new level of awareness?
- How many kids do you want to correctly respond to questions about fire safety?

For the smoking cessation example, one outcome will be those who say they are committed to quitting and reflect that they have an understanding as to how. Another will be how many have successfully stopped smoking by the end of the series of sessions. Even more telling will be how many remain nonsmokers six months later.

Benchmarks

Benchmarks, also called indicators, are measurable milestones toward your outcomes. If you want to increase the number of people who utilize your services by 600 over the next year, how many need to do so in the next 90 days?

If you want 50 percent of people in your smoking cessation workshop to continue refraining from smoking six months later, what percentage will need to be doing so one month later?

Benchmarks help you compare how your outputs and activities are doing in relation to what you seek to achieve, how you are progressing toward your end goals. They help guide your program and determine if you need to course correct in order to reach your goal (or perhaps adjust the goal up or down depending on how things are going). You don't want to wait until the end of the year to figure out that everyone in your smoking cessation class has gone back to the habit. Or never stopped in the first place.

Phase Overview

No matter what kind of measurement program you take on, or how nuanced your mission, there are certain basic steps that will get you to the end goal of learning the effectiveness of your programs.

Specifically, there are four primary steps, and several steps within them, that make up your measurement program. We begin with an overview, and then will explore each area.

Stick with me on this. It won't be as painful as you might think.

Phase 1: Set them up.
- Determine the goals of your outcome measurement project.
- Identify which programs you will evaluate.
- Decide who will be involved and the timeline for the project.
- Identify the outcomes you want to measure.
- Select the indicators that will identify progress toward outcomes.
- Determine what data you will collect and how you will do it.

Phase 2: Get them in.
- Gather the data and information.

Phase 3: Get them out.
- Analyze them.

Phase 4: Use them.
- Report them.
- Improve your services.

Many programs follow this structure, or something close. Now, doesn't that feel better already?

Chapter 48

PHASE 1: SET THEM UP

Get ready to set the goals of your measurement program. Chances are that you have several reasons for developing outcomes measures. These may include:

- Sincerely wanting to learn about the effectiveness of your programs so you can improve upon them and ensure funding is being used as efficiently as possible.
- Fulfilling the grant requirement that you record and report back specific measures.
- Reporting the outcomes to your board, donors, and other stakeholders to get them to understand your impact, then give of their time or money (again).
- Using the measures for staff morale and training.

A WORD ON STAFF

Don't assume your staff will understand or embrace your outcome measurement project just because you decided to take it on. Let them know ahead of time why you're making measurement a priority, and get them on board. Do not be apologetic or roll your eyes when you talk about taking time and resources to do this. Instead, be enthusiastic. They will follow your lead.

Now, let's tackle the concrete steps of setting up your program.

Step 1: Identify which programs you will evaluate.
There are two ways to go when creating a program to measure the effectiveness of your programs.

You can begin with just one program, or you can begin with a set of programs that are similar enough in their process and services that they will most likely have similar outcomes and indicators.

For example, you can choose just one of your residential programs within your housing department. Or you can look at them all collectively, since they all lead toward a similar, greater purpose.

The benefit of choosing just one program is that you can use it as a pilot to test your organization's readiness for this kind of work. You will also most likely get the outcomes of the particular project more quickly, which will allow you to use them more quickly, and perhaps even gain funding support for the rest of the outcomes project.

The negative to choosing only one program at a time is that the whole outcome measurement project will take considerably longer. You may also find yourself approaching the same stakeholders over time (through surveys and other instruments) on different programs. They might get fatigued or even annoyed.

No matter which way you go, just be intentional about your choice.

Step 2: Decide who will be involved and the timeline for the project.
Once you figure out which program or programs you want to evaluate, you need to determine the players who will be involved and the timeline for the project.

You'll want to determine which managers will be involved, and then which program staff. These are your experts and will have the most intimate knowledge of the services you provide.

It's often helpful to pick a lead, and then create a committee with several people tackling different pieces of the project. The committee structure also helps to hold the players accountable to the process and timeline.

At this stage you will also want to consider whether or not you want to extend outside of your staff for committee members. The good news is that your donors, volunteers, or board members will have a different perspective and will bring an external set of knowledge and experiences to the table. The bad news? Once you ask for their feedback, you have to honor it, respect it, and use it, even if you don't want to in the end.

Finally, you might also want to engage some external help to coordinate the administrative or data pieces. Students are a great resource to help you move your process forward. There are plenty of academic programs that involve measurement, research, and evaluation, and the students need real-life experience. That's just what you've got.

As far as the timeline, set the amount of time the project deserves, enough for all of the tasks you will need to get done. Don't rush through it, but don't let it stretch on indefinitely either. Not only will the information you collect become antiquated, but the process as a whole might just drive you crazy.

Step 3: Identify the outcomes of the programs you want to measure.
Once you've figured out the programs you will measure, you need to identify the outcomes for each one.

Remember, *outcomes* are the results of the program, the impacts and changes that occur for the client as a result of the program. They are *not* the activities completed as part of the process.

Outcomes often begin with words like *increase, enhance, create,* or *reduce.* For example, an outcome of our HIV prevention program was an increased level of education, awareness, and healthy choices around risky behavior.

Know that outcome creation is much easier to define for some programs than others. A weight loss program lends itself nicely to outcome measure development, as an obvious outcome is client weight loss. An organization that creates theatrical productions might look at attendance at their events, and whether or not it goes up or down.

Other programs, like the HIV example above, are trickier. In these cases it's tempting to measure the wrong things: the number of flyers distributed or the number of participants in educational workshops. While these are both important to understanding the process, they won't say whether or not the program itself worked.

Creating these outcomes can be challenging and messy. There are no hard rules. They will differ based on your programs or goals. The best thing you can do is truly think through what you want your program to *do* for those you serve in the end, and create outcomes around that concept.

One other point to make this whole thing easier: While your program has its own specific parameters and nuances, chances are somebody has done this before for a program similar to yours. There is no need to start from scratch. Do your research and find what other organizations have done. Then start there, and customize to suit your needs.

Step 4: Select the indicators that will identify progress toward outcomes.
Now that you know what you're trying to achieve, you need to figure out how you'll know when you've achieved it.

Indicators, or benchmarks, track progress toward your defined outcomes. They tend to focus on numbers and percentages.

For example, an indicator of the weight loss program could be that 75 percent of clients lose weight in the first two weeks of participation in the program. Another focus could take it even further, stating that 75 percent of clients are halfway to their weight loss goal within six months of participation.

For our HIV prevention program, 80 percent of participants needed to leave a presentation demonstrating an increased knowledge of HIV risk by performing better on a written test at the end of the session than they did at the start.

Like the outcomes themselves, these will never be perfect. They don't come from some kind of textbook. Do your best by thinking through the question of *how you will know* when your audience is progressing toward your outcome, and try to set up indicators that are feasible.

As with everything else, you will most likely have to tweak these along the way to ensure you are getting useful information, and to readjust so that your indicators are not too easy or challenging. Just try not to do this too often, as it makes it harder to gauge your progress over time.

Step 5: Determine what data you will collect and how you will do it.
If you are not an evaluation wonk, this could be the one that gets you a bit intimidated. Don't let it.

As with the other components of measurement, this is both art and science—and you know more than you think you do.

We explore the options around data collection in the next section. Just make sure that as you set your strategy up, this is a component you think through beforehand.

Chapter 49

PHASE 2: GET THEM IN

When determining the methods you will use to gather information, the choices might seem endless. Some are relatively simple, some decidedly more technical in nature. Think through them all as you consider what you want to learn and who you need to reach to get there. Often, a mix of a few techniques will help you get a comprehensive picture of your progress toward outcomes.

Option 1: Do a file review.
One simple option to begin your information-gathering process is to review the very files and program records that already exist in your organization. They will tell you a lot. In the example of the weight loss program, for example, they will tell you how many weight loss clients are progressing toward your benchmarks at any given time.

The trick here, of course, is to make sure that the paperwork is set up and completed, and files are maintained over time. This means you need to clearly communicate your expectations with program staff, including the policies, procedures, and systems as to how and how often the files will be completed and organized. If your staff sees this as a priority and knows they will be held accountable for client records, they are much more likely to complete their records before leaving the office for the day. And they are less likely to save it all for a Friday at 4 p.m., which leaves room for all kinds of errors.

Option 2: Observe.

Ongoing observation over time also works for some programs. If an environmental organization is trying to keep litter down at local beaches, setting up a regular and formal way to observe this and measuring progress over time can be a helpful way to monitor progress toward that outcome.

Option 3: Conduct surveys, interviews, and focus groups.

We now move to data collection methods that require a bit more planning and work.

They often require collecting information specific to your evaluation strategy, with the goal of measuring progress in a concrete way. These kinds of techniques include client and customer surveys, interviews, and focus groups.

Here are some thing to keep in mind:

- Get maximized information from each instrument.

Surveys, interviews, and focus groups can actually get at a number of different outcomes, including changes in knowledge, behavior, and actions. At the same time, you can use these instruments to test overall client satisfaction and need.

While this section is really about measuring true outcomes, that doesn't mean the other information is not useful. Just be coordinated about how you gather it and utilize the opportunity thoughtfully. Think through both what you want to measure and what other information might be helpful to you as you work to move your organization forward. Create one set of surveys that meets all your needs so that clients aren't inundated with a number of different evaluation techniques throughout the year.

- Keep them simple.

While you want to get as much information as possible from each technique, you need to keep the instruments simple. This will not only help your clients when completing the information, but also help you analyze the information later. The last thing you need is more data than you can handle after the information is in. Be thoughtful and inclusive, but also be choosy and strategic with your questions.

- Coordinate among and between your programs.

As you create your information-gathering system, consider which programs you will target, and if it makes sense to gather data on more than one program within a department, or even among a few different departments. It you do gather data from more than one department, again, just make sure the instrument is simple, clear, and consistent. If the questions were written by different people in different departments, the people filling out the surveys should not be able to tell.

Answer a few other questions before beginning.

- *Should we pilot?*

It is common for new instruments to include some glitches, to miss some questions, or to include pieces that just don't make sense. Testing your instruments on a small, concentrated portion of the target audience will get at these issues before you launch. It's an extra step, yes, but it might save you time and headaches later on.

- *How often will we gather new information?*

Collecting information on your outcomes regularly and through a set schedule will get you long-term results. You may want to consider collecting information before, during, and then after the client is engaged.

For example, when we provided housing services to our clients, we monitored their medical statistics when they first came into the program, several months after they were housed, and then six months after that. Our program wasn't just about fixing their housing crisis, but about seeing if the program helped them get healthier, and then sustained that health in the long run.

- *How will we ensure confidentiality?*

A trusting relationship with those you serve is the most important thing you've got. Consider the need for confidentiality before you begin your process, and then all along the way.

If you serve clients in any kind of sensitive capacity, consent forms may be required. Even if you don't, you'll want to assure participants that their information will be held in confidence, then make sure you do everything possible to ensure this. If you are working with audiences where the information can feasibly made public, make sure you let participants know.

Chapter 50

PHASE 3: GET THEM OUT

If you've determined your outcomes, identified your benchmarks, and gathered meaningful information through one or more methods, let's pause here so I can give you a big, mental pat on the back.

You've come far—farther than many, many nonprofits.

Now, the next thing is to get that outcome information out in a way that's meaningful.

Begin by going back to where you started: the goals of your evaluation program. Keep your outcomes and indicators in mind as you look at the data. It will help you focus on the information that is most meaningful to you, such as the changes in behavior, the improvements in blood tests, or the number of people who are now nonsmokers.

That being said, you will most likely also discover information and themes you hadn't even thought of, that don't necessarily relate to any of the goals you set. Perhaps a group of people in your weight loss program show that they've reduced their consumption of alcohol because your workshops focus on overall wellness. Think of this information as a bonus and be sure to make note of it. Consider formally gathering data around these emerging issues.

Now, to analyzing the data.

Don't let that word scare you, and don't stop now. You've got this.

Step 1: Tabulate.
When working with quantitative data created through instruments like surveys with yes/no or ranking questions, or a review of information in client files, begin by simply tabulating that information. Create a spreadsheet that reflects the questions and enter the

information. (This is one great place to utilize a volunteer or an intern. Just make sure you've addressed the issue of confidentiality.)

Look at trends by calculating data averages, means, and ranges (knowing that you might need to look for any skewing of information based on the feedback of just one or two people).

But don't stop there.

You will also want to tabulate and record the qualitative data—things like verbal responses to interviews or focus group questions or written survey comments. Look for themes and trends, then group the answers when you tabulate them.

Step 2: Read it.
Next? Hunker down and read it all.

This may seem obvious, but it can be a pretty tedious task. It can also be hard to read honest feedback from your clients, complete with their subjective, editorialized, and often critical comments. But you need to know it all.

Again, look for trends. If clients repeatedly relate a certain difficulty in accessing services, or if a common barrier to achieving the programmatic goals emerges, reflect that. If you find that patrons simply don't attend your theater productions on a certain weekday, that's important to know. So is learning that your smoking cessation program participants tend to relapse right around the fifth session.

Step 3: Organize it.
Once everything is tabulated, organize it. Put the information into context, comparing actual results with your indictors to identify gaps or successes. You can also compare it to best practices or common standards for similar programs, national trends, outcomes borrowed from collaborative partners, et cetera. You may also consider breaking the information out further, for instance based on the demographics, geographical area of residence, and various logistics of the program itself.

The more perspective and context you use when looking at your data, the better. Information on its own isn't nearly as meaningful as when you compare it to your goals, your benchmarks, or the outcomes of others.

Step 4: Ask staff to review it—but be careful.

Select one or more members of your program staff to interpret the outcome data from their area. This will not only utilize your internal experts, but will also continue to get staff invested in the process of evaluation. Talk to staff about the data and whether or not it reflects what they expected or understood the program's effectiveness to be.

A caveat: When you do this, be sure to let them know this is not about evaluating *their* abilities. This isn't about validating their work. It's about making sure their programs are creating as much impact as possible. As with everything else, your choice of words will be key in effectively getting the results you need, in keeping them invested in this project, and in boosting staff morale.

Step 5: Understand it.

Ask staff to reflect not just on the information that's in line with your indicators or your thinking, but also on the information that surprises you.

If some trending just does not seem correct to you, or is markedly different from what you thought would be the case, you must seek to understand it. Look at both those results that are substantially better than your indicators and those that come in far behind.

Though you and your staff might be tempted to disregard the latter, don't. It's too easy to get defensive and shut down. Instead, work with staff (and perhaps your participants) to gain an understanding of the reasons behind it.

Even though you might be tempted, even though you and your staff have the most expertise on your organization, do not skip this step. In the end, this kind of information could be most valuable to you in gaining a new perspective on the effectiveness of your programs or the challenges facing your clients.

Now, despite my point above, it is possible that the gaps or surprises result from the data itself being inaccurate. There will be factors that impact the information and its trending, and, as long as you don't always go there first as the reason for outcomes you don't like, you will want to consider them.

For instance…

- *There may have been flaws in the instrument.*

It could be that your survey wasn't clear, or that some of the questions included more than one meaning for various clients or participants. It could be that the questions you asked in the interview or focus group were particularly personal or involved a level of self-reporting that caused some people to answer less honestly. (These are the kinds of issues that you'll discover if you pilot the instrument with your target audience first.)

- *Your budget or staffing changed.*

If you review information from year to year, or even from when you began the process to the end, you may have experienced programmatic changes along the way. Perhaps you had to cut a case manager at your health clinic or decrease the number of scholarships available for your education program. This could skew the results of the data and its accompanying trends. Chances are you will know this beforehand, and can keep an eye out for these discrepancies.

- *External factors impacted your organizational effectiveness.*

My mother always used to say that life is what happens when we're busy making other plans.

Once you choose a period of time and a strategy to gather data, things will happen. Food bank usage goes up around the holidays, a new program on pollution comes out right before you test knowledge about the environment, or the economy tanks just as you're testing the ability of your organization to place people in permanent jobs.

Factors like this will impact the outcomes of your program. Think them through ahead of time as best you can, then just do your best. You know a lot intuitively, so you'll know if these factors are truly causing skewed results or if you're using them as an excuse to disregard the results you don't like.

• *People like you a lot—or don't.*

Some people can't wait for the opportunity to sing the praises of your program or, conversely, get out their frustrations. They might use your evaluation tool to do just that.

Take both with a grain of salt, but in this case, try to make it a small one.

Chapter 51

PHASE 4: USE THEM

Once you get the data out, use them.

Far too often I see nonprofits put together some kind of evaluation program, usually based on funding requirements, dutifully fill out the funder's reporting spreadsheet, and then move on.

It's a huge, missed opportunity. When you have created a strategic outcome measurement program, there are a number of ways to use that data, both internally and externally. Take advantage of them all. It would be a shame—a waste—not to do so.

How to Use Your Outcomes

There are two primary ways you can, and should, use your outcome measurement information.

Way 1. To get better.

Of course, the primary reason for evaluating your programs is to make those programs better. By using an objective means to gauge the effectiveness, strengths, and challenges of your services, you force yourself and those around you to recognize it all. When the information is ready, bring your program staff together and go over it. Discuss it all: the outcomes, the successes, and the surprises. And know that your communication here, as in every other aspect of your organization, will be critical to how this information is received and acted upon over time.

- Begin where you started, letting staff in on why you started this outcome measurement work in the first place.

- Emphasize that the goal of everyone, every day, is to make sure the mission is carried out as effectively as possible.
- Remind staff that this is not about evaluating certain programs for continuation (unless it is) or evaluating the effectiveness of certain staff (unless it is). This is about your continued commitment to excellence.

When you communicate outcomes that didn't measure up the way you thought they would, be especially careful with your words. It's hard enough for a staff member to know he or she hasn't performed up to expectations when it's between the two of you in a room. It's even harder when it's in front of the person's peers and then reported to others. Do your best to de-personalize. Discuss the results in terms of the program, not the individuals running it. If you do have concerns about those individuals based on the outcomes, address them, but do so one-on-one.

Conversely, if a staff member has clearly been pivotal in reaching and exceeding benchmarks, it's okay, appropriate, and good policy to reward that person for it. Recognition goes far, and if staff members see that the successes of others are being noted in some way, it's some extra motivation to work even harder.

Consider using your outcomes to encourage innovation. Assess the results and play with new ideas to make them better or enhance them. Based on what you see, there will be opportunities to improve and enhance, to brainstorm ideas and then execute a few. Perhaps you can make a few small changes and test them out on a specific group of clients, then bring the results back to the group for continued discussion.

This kind of strategic, innovative discussion can go far for your programs, as well as for your staff investment and morale.

Way 2. To get support.
This is your chance to show others you're doing good *well*. It is almost a crime to evaluate your organization and not let others in on it.

You stand out from your competition simply by creating a

strategic evaluation initiative. That in itself is impressive. Now, take it a step further and let your stakeholders know how things are going.

Begin by writing a report…but be careful. You are reporting results to staff, board, and external stakeholders, not to evaluation scientists or data lovers. This means that, as with everything else, you need to write your information in a way that is clear, interesting, and succinct. Write for your audience. (See page 220.)

Trust me, people will be impressed and engaged if you do this right—if you provide them with information that is interesting and that will not take a significant amount of time or translation to read.

When creating the report…

- Think about what your readers might most want to learn, and focus on that. Perhaps even ask a few of them what they might find most compelling before you begin.
- Summarize throughout your report, and consider starting with an executive summary.
- Include both clear quantitative data and analyzed qualitative information.
- Make sure you let people know what you learned and what you intend to do with the information. And then do it.

Think of your report as a marketing tool, because it is. You might need to create a few different versions of the document for different audiences, and that's okay.

Just remember, write for the audience. You might want to include all kinds of detailed data just because you love your organization so much. That will not work. Extraneous details, densely packed-in paragraphs, and itty-bitty margins will only cause people to put the report down and move on to something else.

Once you've got the report, use it like nobody's business.

- Create simple presentations and go on the road with your information. Present findings to your full staff and include appropriate programmatic personnel. Present them to the board and do the same. The more you inform these critical stakeholders, the more they can carry the messages on to others.

- Make sure your funders know more than they asked for. They are used to seeing their required information, but not much else. It will be a breath of fresh air—if you write succinctly and in an interesting way—to expand beyond that.
- Bring the information to current and prospective donors. By clearly showing the impact you are making with their money, you are creating an extremely compelling case for new or continued support. And again, you are standing out from the other organizations who are also hitting them up, but who are doing so without the data that prove they are both strategic and effective.
- Include the information in your annual report and on your website.

Your information presents an incredible opportunity. When used correctly, it is gold.

A FEW WORDS ON REPORTING NEGATIVE INFORMATION

It might be tempting for you to omit outcomes that aren't as positive as you would like. If there are only a few among many positive outcomes, I encourage you to think otherwise. Including some room for improved performance will make the whole report more credible because your stakeholders will know you're not hiding anything.

If the majority of your outcomes illustrate a level of underperformance, then you've got bigger problems, and reporting is not where you want to focus at the moment. Instead, go back to my point about using your outcomes to make your programs better, think through the reasons for so many negative indicators, and address them. Chances are they reflect an issue with your organizational strategy, your program, your people, or a combination.

Even if this is the case and you focus on fixing your problems, for the time being, hold on to the data. When you address these issues and begin to resolve them, the great thing is your new outcomes will reflect your ability to take a flawed program and fix it.

Chapter 52

WHEN TO GO OUTSIDE

Now that I've potentially convinced you that you do not need to engage an outside consultant to take on the entire outcome measurement program, I will say that there may be times when it is appropriate to bring in a certain level of expertise.

As you consider doing so, just make sure you are doing it for the right reasons—not because you're intimidated and not because measurement bores you.

Six Reasons to Engage Outside Support

Reason 1. You don't know your goals.
As I've discussed, the first thing you need to know in figuring out what you're measuring is what you're making progress *toward*.

Too often we try to evaluate our programs in a vacuum, figuring out how we are impacting those we serve when we don't know how many people we're aiming for or how we truly plan to serve them. We strive to measure client satisfaction when we don't know what we want them to be satisfied about or what kind of results we feel are reasonable.

The best way to know your organizational goals is to create a strategic plan that clearly defines them. If you don't have one, get one—and not just to make your measurement strategies more effective. No organization should be without a true, living strategic plan. Outside consultants can be used to help you create one.

Reason 2. You want help getting the data in.
Chances are you'll use a number of different vehicles to gather your data, some of it significantly easier to use than others. These include everything from file audits and programmatic observation to surveys and focus groups. (See page 262.)

You know that any kind of communication with your clients and other stakeholders should be done with absolute care. You don't want to hit up these individuals too often, and you want any information you get from them to be useful.

If you are reaching out to clients who might not be forthcoming, if you are trying to gather information on more than one item or with more than one goal in mind, or if you feel that you're not quite sure how to phrase questions that will get you the information you want, this is an appropriate time to bring someone in. A consultant can help you evaluate your ideas, questions, and goals, and make sure you are squeezing every last possible bit of information out of your instruments—without overwhelming the participants.

TWO WORDS OF WISDOM

Using someone from the outside doesn't give you an excuse to skip your part. Make sure you provide the consultant with the information required to get you what you need. It will be a lot cheaper than asking someone to start from scratch.

Also, be clear that you do not want to figure out world peace. While you want to make your instruments as efficient as possible, you also want to be very focused on what you need to know to assess your organization's impact. Don't use your instruments to get ancillary information that you really won't use. You can find out how your clients feel about the temperature in your lobby a different way. Evaluators can get carried away in creating instruments and may want to help you measure things that are not significant to your overall strategy. There's no greater barrier to getting people to respond to your questions than asking too many of them or making the inquiries too scientific.

Remember, you know your stakeholders best. Bring your own expertise to the table, articulate your goals, and be the leader of this partnership. Use the evaluator to get the instruments right, not to coordinate your program.

Reason 3. You want help figuring out the data.

Collecting data and determining trends can be somewhat simple. The analysis piece is where things can get tricky.

- There may be nuanced answers resulting from focus groups, and you need to determine whether they are statistically relevant.
- Your survey might address a number of your programs, and you're having a hard time determining which pieces are related to which services.
- You might find it especially difficult to distinguish between your outcomes and your outputs. You might be too close to the material. It might be too complex.

The analysis component is important. It's where a lot of the proverbial rubber meets a lot of the proverbial road. You're not just gathering information on a program; you are trying to make decisions about it. You need to know what's working and what's not—and if it is working at all.

If the analysis piece is tripping you up, then look for that specific skill set in an evaluator.

Reason 4. Objectivity is not your organization's strength.

Are you truly ready to hear what is working and—often much more difficult—what is not? Is this organization your baby? Are you a founder? Can you hear critique—the negative kind?

It's important to know this about yourself, both for this process and just in general as you strive to adapt your organization to the inevitable changing needs in your community. Bringing in someone from the outside can help—both to make sure you're not skewing your results in a way that feels better to you and to help you report the negative stuff to those stakeholders who might not be able or willing to hear it.

Reason 5. You truly don't have the time.
Evaluation of your programs needs to happen. I think I've emphasized this point. If you are in the midst of a number of projects, trying to balance your budget and get grant dollars in the door, and working to recruit effective new board members, you simply might not have time to spearhead this effort.

And if your staff also doesn't have the time—or, worse, you don't trust them to get it done—then getting outside help is appropriate.

But...

Just know that we can all find ways to be busy every day. Emails are always there and our staff can always use guidance. The sinks will leak and the server will shut down. Don't let the minutia of the day-to-day give you the excuse to bail out of this important role if you can at all help it.

Reason 6. You have funding.
These days, funders have not only bought into the importance of outcome measurement, they often require it. The good ones often fund it.

If you're lucky enough to be the recipient of funding for evaluation, you of course will want to take advantage of it. Bring in someone to set up the process, define the goals, implement some of the vehicles, and help you analyze and report the data.

But...

There are two things to keep in mind here.

First, make sure you have a say in who will be working with you.

Funders love to suggest consultants, and that's often very helpful. At the same time, you need to make sure the consultant is the right fit for the organization and for you.

Second, you want to have the opportunity to work with the consultant on the entirety of your outcome measurement needs, not just the program the funder is providing dollars for. Have these discussions with your funder before the process starts. It will make the process a whole lot easier.

How to Choose the Right Consultant

There many kinds of consultants, and chances are you'll have a good number of options. The important thing is to engage in this relationship strategically and effectively (see page 110).

Some evaluation professionals will come from a large firm with a whole lot of expertise, and as a result, a hefty price tag. Some will be just one- or two-person shops, and might be more targeted to certain pieces of the process.

There are also plenty of academic programs on evaluation, and students eager to do some real-life work. Many will be required to take on a project for submission. You can also utilize these students as interns.

The most important thing, of course, is to find the right option to meet your previously determined project goals, your budget, and your time constraints. Do not save a buck by bringing in an undergrad when you need a comprehensive outcome measurement plan. Do not bring in some fancy, costly firm when you need someone to help create a survey for you. Be intentional.

Chapter 53

THE ROLE OF QUALITATIVE MEASUREMENT

I've been pretty quantitative in my measurement-speak so far, and there's a reason why: That kind of data is often the piece that's missing. Nonprofits tend to be much more focused on the qualitative stuff.

No doubt about it, nonprofits have great stories to share—of client impact and inspirational donors and incredible advocates. And because they have these stories, and because it's easy to wrap your head around the use of them, the organization doesn't just focus on them—it focuses *only* on them. And that's not good enough.

That being said, there is definitely a place for qualitative information, the kind that comes from anecdotes and endorsements. This type of information also needs to play a role in your outcome measurement strategy, your decision making, and your communication to your stakeholders. After all, if you are trying to improve people's lives in some way through your organization, it only makes sense to include the stories of these people as part of your measure of success.

There are many ways to gather this kind of information. As with everything else, it just takes some planning ahead of time, and a process that you have others follow to ensure it's done effectively.

One way to get qualitative information at the same time you're getting the harder data is to ask for additional comments in your surveys and for examples in your focus groups. They will not only help you identify trends of what is working and what is not, but they will also provide great information for you to use in your marketing materials. (Just be sure to ask for permission to use people's stories before you do so, and, if appropriate, offer them anonymity or the opportunity to change their names.)

It's actually helpful to gather qualitative data all year long. Have an area on your website where people can submit their comments. Add a few open-ended questions about why people value your organization to your donor and volunteer forms.

Get into the habit of inviting feedback—at lunch meetings and donor receptions, at site visits and networking events. Mark down the really good responses, or ask people to follow up with an email that lays out what they've said. Most people love being asked their opinions on things (see page 169), and you won't just get some great information to use and share, but will also be building relationships with your stakeholders.

Of course, when you ask for feedback, you need to be sure you're ready to hear it. And when you do, and it's not what you want to hear, resist being defensive or explaining yourself to the person offering the information. That's a great way to make your process—and your relationship—appear insincere.

Go Beyond Your Comfort Zone

One more word on this point.

Be sure to ask more than just your greatest fans for their opinions. It is tempting to go to those who think you're great. It is also tempting to avoid those who might have some more critical feedback. And while it's probably not worthwhile to ask your biggest enemies for their opinions, there are plenty of others from whom you can learn.

You know your organization best, and you will know when something is valid or people are just venting. Take it all in, thank people for their feedback, and objectively assess their input so that you can act on it appropriately.

And if the feedback makes you mad, wait until you're back in the car *after* the lunch meeting to roll your eyes.

Chapter 54

WHAT NEXT?

So you've completed your outcome measurement initiative. You've determined your goals and created benchmarks. You've developed a program that involves your stakeholders appropriately and gets your staff behind it. You've collected the results, analyzed them, and reported them far and wide. You have taken full advantage of the fact that you are a strategic leader, and you believe one of the most important things you can do for your organization is truly understand your impact and then adapt it to do even greater things in the future.

Congratulations!

No, I mean it. If you have done even one thing from the paragraph above, you are to be commended. You understand the Mission Myth and you are dedicated to putting time and resources into elements of your organization that are not sexy, but still so very important. You are also willing to be introspective.

You are a leader. But I knew that.

And don't forget, you are so far ahead of so many other nonprofits that your funders, partners, donors, volunteers, and community members cannot help but be impressed.

So go ahead and celebrate. You deserve it.

But...

Do not cross this project off your list and think it is done. This is not the end, but the beginning of something great.

You have built the foundation for a process that will carry you far into the future. You will use the outcomes you've built to measure your progress next year, maybe sooner. You will find that your donors and other stakeholders will come to get used to your meaningful outcomes. Continue to be the leader in your community on outcome measurement. And know that the project will be so much easier the next time.

One final note on your future outcome measurement efforts:

Adjust the goals and vehicles as you go as appropriate, but don't reinvent that proverbial wheel each time. Keeping some of it the same will help you consistently measure things over time.

Tweak, yes. But don't recreate if you can help it, no matter what your newest board member, new funder, or new consultant wants you to do.

And seriously… nicely done.

PART SIX

WRAPPING IT UP

Chapter 55

YOUR MISSION MATTERS

Your mission matters. It's the whole reason you work at your organization. It's why you go through the challenges, face the crises, ask for the money, and maneuver so many stakeholder relationships each and every day.

It's what makes it all worth it.

And now you know that your mission matters so much that sometimes you need to turn your attention *away* from it to focus on what will help you achieve it most successfully.

And sometimes this will make you the bad guy. Sometimes this means sacrificing a production, a workshop, a portion of rental assistance for a client, in the name of a new server, an effective website, or paying the right people to get the job done.

When you make these kinds of decisions, people will balk. They will feel uncomfortable. They will think you don't understand.

Focusing on the four *M*s does not mean you don't care. It means you care so much that you are willing to do everything you can to make sure the mission isn't just doing good, but doing good *well*.

The four *M*s may not seem sexy. They may not seem altruistic. They often don't seem like any fun. But you know they are critical in achieving your goals. They control whether or not you serve your community. And in the end, they determine whether you succeed or fail.

I've spent some time thinking about how to end this book.

I've tried to spend our time together validating you for all your hard and uniquely challenging work, putting some things in perspective, and perhaps getting you to think a bit differently about the priorities of running a nonprofit.

I also know I've been somewhat hard on you.

I believe nonprofits, like everything else, often need tough love to come to the reality that focusing on mission alone, letting emotions get in the way, acting less than strategically, thinking with the heart only and leaving the head out of it—all of this is a disservice.

I know that you understand this. I know, just by the fact that you made it this far, that you love your work, you are passionate about your mission, and you want to do it better.

I also know that chances are you're not celebrating enough of your successes and that in general you're probably pretty hard on yourself. And, if you're doing even some of the things described in these pages, you are or will most likely be less popular as a result.

You already know that staff and volunteers and board members love to focus on mission. So when you put some of these concepts in motion, when you set as priorities things like policies and procedures, outcome measurement, and donor management, others might believe it is not what you're supposed to be doing. That you're not doing your job.

Please let me assure you that you are.

You are honoring your organization and creating a new level of excellence by making the hard decisions, having the difficult discussions, acting as a leader, and keeping every single proverbial ball in the air.

The other thing to know is that you will make mistakes. Not everything will go well, and sometimes you will miss the days of the more random use of your time, answering emails and calls as they come in, letting anybody walk in your office and take up your time, acting as the almighty cheerleader instead of the critical combination of inspired leader, excellent manager, and accountability mechanism.

When you make these mistakes, I implore you…let them go.

Learn from them, yes…then let them go.

You are doing hard work, some of the hardest there is. It's also some of the loneliest. You are juggling duties nobody else can truly understand, managing the most politically difficult relationships there are, keeping track of your money, and being your organization's effective ambassador. You are making sure the organization is doing good *well*.

It is incredible work. Is it also fulfilling in its successes? You bet.

But it will take its toll on you.

Chances are it already has. Hang in there. And know that you're accomplishing amazing things.

And Finally...

I now want to thank you.

Thank you for spending time learning some lessons you might not have known before. Thank you for working to make yourself better at your critical job, to make yourself a better leader. Thank you for committing to running your nonprofit better, so that you can achieve your mission better.

I promise you, you *are* a leader. You know more than you think you do. You will be more and more successful. You will make a difference.

Now, go do good. And do it *well*.

INDEX

ACKNOWLEDGMENTS

My mother likes to say that she might not have a grandchild, but she's got a grandbook.

It feels like a fitting analogy. Having never been through any kind of birthing ritual, I can't say for sure which is the greater test on the body, mind, and spirit. What I do know is that the process of facing the soaring highs and gut-wrenching lows from my time as executive director of Colorado AIDS Project, combined with the need to dig deep in order to write, edit, and promote this book, has been one of the most fulfilling, exhilarating, vulnerable challenges I've faced so far.

The book in your hands (or on your screen) simply wouldn't be there if not for the support, validation, strong shoulders, and ongoing grace of the following people:

To Julian Rush, who spent 18 years making Colorado AIDS Project into the kind of organization someone like me could take over, dig into, and build up.

To Tom Buche, for telling me I'd be a great ED, then making sure I got my chance to be one...and to David Alexander, whose sage advice and dazzling smile guided me through my earliest ED crises.

To Bob Nogueira and Rich Corbetta, who proved that a relationship with your board president can be not just effective, but delightful.

To Robert George, who provided me with hearty belly-laughs all the way through seven years of organizational crises, heartache, and near catastrophes.

To Nan Clydesdale, who taught me how to be a *good bad guy*, then stood by me whenever I had to be one.

To Karla Olson, my book sherpa, who guided me through a writing process filled with self-doubt, perfectionism, and all kinds of lessons on what it takes to get your book out to the world and into welcoming hands...and for setting me straight on my obsession with ellipses.

To Joe Lawlor, my buddy, writing partner, validator, honest critic, and faithful friend.

To Vasi Huntalas, my coach, who spent the last year reminding me that I'm still a good person even if my book stinks...and to Sue Carter Kahl, who read the whole thing before anybody else just so she could tell me it doesn't.

To Bernice Bruno and Fran Sciuto, who join me every morning to build up our bodies, which in turn allows us to clear our minds, energize our spirits, and strengthen our souls

To the folks at the Brickyard Coffee & Tea, whose daily dose of vanilla nut brew, warm smiles, and internet-free space led directly to the completion of this book.

To my mother, Patricia Costa, who to this day continues to provide me with one of the greatest gifts of a lifetime: knowing that I am loved – purely and wholly and unquestionably – each and every day on this earth.

To my father, Thomas Maloney, who taught me to drive ferociously toward the things that matter, and let go of the things that don't.

And to husband, my Jay, my partner in this never-ending slumber party, for sharing in a life that would be blissful even if I never had a book to call my own -- and for slogging through hundreds of discussions about writer's block, subtitle choices, cover options, and marketing strategies.

It is a powerful, humbling, blessed thing to be able to count so many extraordinary people as part of this journey. I am exceedingly grateful to each one for holding me up when I could no longer take it, and standing aside when I needed to find my own way.

ABOUT THE AUTHOR

Deirdre Maloney got her job as the executive director of a multi-million dollar nonprofit organization at a relatively young age. At 28 years old, she found herself running Colorado AIDS Project in Denver, Colorado. Seven years later, she emerged from the role a confident, self-assured, leader, one who left behind an organization that was stronger, more effective, and functioning more efficiently than ever before.

How did she do it? By making mistakes and learning from each one. By being willing to make unpopular choices for the good of her business. By embracing the harsh truth - that it is only when the nonprofit sector embraces a meaningful business formula that it truly finds success.

Today, Deirdre proudly runs her company, Momentum, which helps nonprofits meet their missions through better business. Through presentations and instruction, as well as customized services like strategic planning, board development, and marketing, Deirdre works with organizations of all sizes to help them make and keep their momentum for optimal success.

In addition to her work through Momentum, Deirdre teaches marketing for the University of San Diego's School of Leadership and Education Sciences. Her writings and articles have appeared in a number of print publications and her blog on leadership has grown steadily in popularity.

Deirdre regularly speaks at conferences around the country. She has become known for saying things that others won't say, for helping nonprofit leaders overcome the challenges facing the sector, and for bringing about a new sense of hope -- for a brighter future, for a better night's sleep.

Deirdre lives in San Diego with her husband, Jay.